Preaching Liberation

Preaching Liberation

James H. Harris

Fortress Press
Minneapolis

Dedicated to my wife and sons
Demetrius Dianetta, James Corey, and Cameron Christopher,
and all who preach the gospel

Preaching Liberation

Scripture quotations from the Revised Standard Version of the Bible are copyright © 1946, 1952, 1971 by the Division of Christian Education of the National Council of the Churches of Christ in the USA and are used by permission. Scripture quotations from the New Revised Standard Version of the Bible are copyright © 1989 by the Division of Christian Education of the National Council of the Churches of Christ in the USA and are used by permission.

Acknowledgements
Go Tell It on the Mountain by James Baldwin, copyright © 1952, 1953 by James Baldwin. Used by permission of Doubleday, a division of Bantam Doubleday, Dell Publishing Group, Inc. "Listen, Lord—A Prayer" and "Let My People Go" from *God's Trombones* by James Weldon Johnson. Copyright © 1927 The Viking Press, Inc., renewed © 1955 by Grace Nail Johnson. Used by permission of Viking Penguin, a division of Penguin Books USA Inc. "Struggling Against the Odds" by James H. Harris, copyright © 1994 Christian Century Foundation. Reprinted from the September-October 1994 issue of *The Christian Ministry*. Used by permission. *The Sanctified Church* by Zora Neale Hurston, copyright © 1983. Reprinted by permission of Turtle Island Foundation. "Preacher Power" by Kephra Burns from *Essence,* copyright © 1989 Essence Communications, Inc. Reprinted by permission. Portions of Chapter 2 previously appeared as "Preaching Liberation: The Afro American Sermon and the Quest for Social Change" printed in the *Journal of Religious Thought,* vol. 46, no. 2, Winter-Spring 1989-90, pp. 72-89. Reprinted by permission.

Cover illustration: . . .*so soll man meinen Bogen sehen in den Wolken* [. . .and the bow is seen in the clouds, Gen 9:14] by Volker Benninghoff, 1970, collection of the artist. Used by permission.

Cover and text designed by Joseph Bonyata

Library of Congress Cataloging-in-Publication Data
Harris, James H., 1952-
    Preaching Liberation / by James H. Harris
      p. cm.—(Fortress resources for preaching)
    Includes bibliographical references.
    ISBN 0-8006-2841-1 (alk. paper)
  1. Afro-American preaching. 2. Liberty—religious aspects—Christianity.
3. Preaching. 4. Liberation Theology. 5. Black theology. I. Title II. Series
BV4208.U6H37 1995
251'.0089'96073—dc20

Manufactured in the U.S.A.   AF 1-2841
01   00   99   98   97   96   95   1   2   3   4   5   6   7   8   9   10

Contents

Preface

Textual preaching that has as its goal the liberation and transformation of individuals and society is the focus of this book.

My context for the practice of ministry is the African American church, which means that this book is culture-based; however, it is not simply a "me-too" effort to discuss oppression and injustice, but an effort to develop a liberation and transformation homiletic that uses the black church experience vis-à-vis Scripture as the foundation for addressing the reality of oppression while simultaneously explicating a methodology that has applicability for all—black, white, red, yellow, and others—who endeavor to preach the gospel. Naturally, the context informs the hermeneutics and exegesis; however, this does not limit or restrict the methodology, which is philosophically grounded in the Hegelian dialectic. The context of the African American church experience is significant to a large number of persons, black and white, who preach the gospel. I have heard persons such as David Buttrick, Richard Lischer, and Fred Craddock "lift up" as models the black preacher and the context of the black church in their lectures; however, they are not necessarily referring to a liberation homiletic, but to a style of preaching they can reference in passing but do not teach in their classes. This book will provide for them and others a paradigm for teaching all of their students, because it is not only a black homiletic, but a transformation and liberation homiletic informed by my own culture and experience. This is the only way that I can authentically and passionately write about preaching, which is so intimately intertwined with my existence. However, I believe that this homiletic transcends black culture to the extent that its use is not limited to any one race of people.

Preaching in some quarters historically has been both an uplifting and transformational enterprise. During slavery, the African American preacher, as God's messenger, was bound by law and custom but was free enough to declare often, in defiance, "what thus saith the Lord." This freedom to speak the truth of the gospel at the risk of being beaten, castrated, sold, or silenced has kept folk praying that the preacher would be protected by God as he endeavored to "break the bread of life." James Weldon Johnson, in his poetic prayer "Listen Lord," captures this spirit of praying for the preacher:

> And now, O Lord, this man of God,
> Who breaks the bread of life this morning—
> Shadow him in the hollow of thy hand,
> And keep him out of the gunshot of the devil.
> Take him, Lord—this morning—
> Wash him with hyssop inside and out,
> Hang him up and drain him dry of sin.
> Pin his ear to the wisdom-post,
> And make his words sledge hammers of truth
> Beating on the iron heart of sin.
> Lord, God, this morning—
> Put his eye to the telescope of eternity,
> And let him look upon the paper walls of time.
> Lord, turpentine his imagination,
> Put perpetual motion in his arms,
> Fill him full of the dynamite of Thy power
> Anoint him all over with the oil of thy salvation,
> And set his tongue on fire![1]

If the preacher's words are to be "sledge hammers of truth," then he or she must deal with the power of the gospel to speak to and to transform individuals as well as the structures of society. This is what transformative preaching is intended to do. It is compelled to address sin and oppression wherever it is found, whether in societal structures or in the consciousness of individuals. I believe that the preacher has struggled historically to do exactly that. Certainly, not everyone who endeavored to preach has been bold enough to confront endemic and pathological problems of racism and oppression, but there have been those who have faced these issues with boldness, ingenuity, and creativity. We all know that a preacher could be killed for being too blunt and forthright during slavery and Jim Crowism. Nevertheless, the tradition of preaching that has inspired, liberated, and transformed persons has a steady line of heralders, from Nat Turner and Henry Highland Garnett to Martin Luther King Jr. and two of my own mentors and teachers, Miles Jones and Samuel D. Proctor.

The cultural context of preaching is the local congregation, with its various levels of social classes, economic conditions, races, and denominations. However, preaching is not limited to any particular local congregation, because, as the church's oldest sustained tradition and activity, it takes place in many contexts—urban, suburban, and rural, from the local church to the entire world community. However, it is cultivated and practiced more in the local church than anywhere else.

I begin with a definition of liberation preaching so that the reader can readily discern that this book is about the process and method of preaching liberation and transformation. A working knowledge of theology as praxis is necessary vis-à-vis understanding black theology as liberation theology. Moreover, I believe it is important to define liberation preaching as preaching in the context of oppression with a view toward liberation.

The liberation preacher has to have a clear theological system that is reflected in every dimension of his or her concept of God. Preaching entails conceptualizing and concretizing the abstract principles of God. This means that there should be a clear theological perspective in every aspect of the preaching message, from the introduction to the conclusion. However, in order for this preaching to qualify as liberation preaching, this perspective should include an emphasis on God's activity in leading a people from oppression to freedom. The liberation preacher needs to have a well defined and understood perspective in each of the major areas of theological discussion: a liberating God and human experience, a liberating God as Jesus Christ, a liberating God and the people of God, and a liberating God and the end of the age. This theological understanding informs the preaching process and determines whether it is indeed liberationist in its focus.

This book is intended for the preacher, theology student, pastor, and theologian, that is, those interested in liberation as a practical concept and in incorporating this concept into the structure and practice of preaching the gospel.

The book closes with a chapter on a methodology for preaching liberation and transformation incorporating context into a dialectic method of sermon construction. In this method, context becomes the antithesis, and the word of God, with its transforming power, becomes the thesis or the ideal. The sermon in its final form becomes the synthesis, because it will reconcile the tension between the context and the scripture.

Acknowledgments

Thanks are extended to the following persons: Samuel D. Proctor, Charles Booth, Edward L. Wheeler, Mac Charles Jones, Michael Nabors, Dwayne Whitehead, Charlotte McSwine, and Robert L. Stephens, who read and provided valuable comments on the entire manuscript; and Rickey Woods, Jerry Gilbert, Joseph Turner, and William Davis were helpful in gathering data on the black church's understanding of liberation and transformation homiletics. All of the members of Second Baptist Church, Richmond, Virginia, helped to make this work possible; however, special thanks to Pearl Mankins, Beatrice Jones, Victoria Bankett, Dorothy Harrison, Verona McLeod, Luther Sadler, Margaret Jones, Effie Rogers, and a host of other church members who provided words of encouragement.

I am grateful to Cain Hope Felder, editor of the *Journal of Religious Thought*, Vol. 46, No. 2, Winter-Spring 1989-90, who first published chapter 2 under the title "Preaching Liberation: The Sermon and the Quest for Social Change" and to Victoria Rebeck of the Christian Century Foundation for first publishing the sermon, "Struggling Against the Odds" after it won an honorable mention in the 1994 Alfred P. Klausler Sermon Awards. The sermon was published in *Christian Ministry*, September-October 1994. Some of this information has been presented under the title "The Theologian as Pastor" during a lecture at the Kelley Miller Smith Institute at Vanderbilt University in October 1992 and during the Martin Luther King Colloquium at Houghton College in Buffalo, New York, where I served as guest lecturer. Special thanks to my homiletics students at the School of Theology, Virginia Union University, Richmond, Virginia. They have taught me a lot and challenged me in developing a pragmatic methodology for textual preaching.

Special thanks and appreciation to my former secretary Evangeline White, who typed the initial document; Patricia D. Cox, my special assistant, who typed and retyped many drafts; and my graduate student Don Pizzeck, who worked on the index for this book. To him, I am very thankful.

As always, my loving wife Demetrius Dianetta and sons James Corey-Alexander and Cameron Christopher-David have inspired my writing; however, I thank God for the grace and strength to do another project of this magnitude!

Introduction:
A Liberation and
Transformation Homiletic

> The black preacher is primarily a prophet who speaks God's truth to the people. The sermon, therefore, is a prophetic oration wherein the preacher "tells it like it is" according to the divine Spirit who speaks through him or her.
> —James H. Cone, *Speaking the Truth*

> "Yes!" cried a woman. . . . "*Tell it!*" "Amen!" cried a voice from far away. "Amen! You preach it boy!" He paused for only a moment and mopped his brow, the heart within him great with fear and trembling, and with power.[2]
> —James Baldwin, *Go, Tell It on the Mountain*

Preaching is the most important act the preacher performs. It is at the center of the black church and its worship experience. It is also "first and foremost a theological act,"[1] because it interprets the meaning of God and Jesus Christ for the believing community. In listing the components of black worship, James Cone, the consummate theologian, lists preaching first, and says, "Next to preaching, song is the most important ingredient in Black worship."[2] Preaching deals with the word of God and how that word speaks to the poor. Moreover, it is the consummate act of interpreting God's word to those who have come to hear the preacher declare in the spirit of the prophets "thus saith the Lord." (Isaiah 1:24; 43:1) Preaching can be described as poetic language used for didactic purposes, or as telling the truth; some will say to the preacher, "You were cooking this morning," to describe the power of the preached word. Others have

1

said, "The Spirit was in here today" or "Pastor, you really helped me in my struggle." James Cone describes the preached word, the sermon, as a "poetic happening, an evocation of an indescribable reality in the lives of people."[3] But it is more than any of these descriptions. It is also retelling the biblical story in an honest, exciting, informative, and engaging way. Yet, it is more than biblical storytelling because the sermon reflects dialogue between contemporary human experience and the message of Scripture. Preaching must be relevant to the needs of our parishioners, addressing issues of life and death as well as social and political questions. It needs to be grounded in the biblical text and the transforming message of Jesus. This means that preaching must be biblically sound and contextually relevant. In the black church, preaching historically has addressed the hurts, needs, and concerns of people who are oppressed.

The preacher is called to preach "in season and out of season." He or she is expected to explain and celebrate the power and wisdom of God in the lives of those who believe. The preacher needs to have a view of God and the world that enables him or her to reconcile the seeming contradictions in life. The preacher's faith in God and his or her understanding of the nature of the human predicament demand that the people of God be informed about and prepared to deal with the issues and troubles of this world. The preacher is a vicarious teacher—one who is constantly engaged in reflection on the practice of Christianity. His or her life and message should reflect the teachings of Christ and the prophets, on one hand, and the experience and culture of black people on the other hand.

Preaching needs to be encouraging, such that the self-esteem of black people is enhanced by understanding the message of Scripture. This means that preaching has to be approached with the highest degree of integrity, respect, and trepidation, because it is an awesome responsibility to tell people how they "ought" to live and what they need to do in order to emulate Jesus of Nazareth. I believe that a theology of preaching is obligated to be wholistic in its focus, that is, to address the potpourri of concerns that engulf the African American community without resorting to a completely psychological, sociological, or cultural analysis of the issues. Preaching needs always to be biblically based; otherwise, it is reduced to secular philosophy or popular religion that is neither compelling nor convicting. But in order for preaching to be more powerful, it must not only be biblically based in a broad sense, but it must be grounded in the textual particulars of the pericope being used.

The preacher is the most visible, listened-to spokesperson in the black community. Unlike other professionals, the preacher has a large number of persons gathered in one place on a weekly basis for the express purpose of hearing "what thus saith the Lord." The opportunity to address those persons' needs in a biblically relevant and serious way is a challenge to all who dare to preach the gospel.

My theology and preaching have been influenced by several pastors and teachers. The Rev. Miles Jones, professor of homiletics at the School of Theology, Virginia Union University, impressed upon me and others that preaching should be kerygmatic, that is, centered on the life, death, and resurrection of Jesus. His method of sermon development is basically correlational or Tillichian. The late John Malcus Ellison, who taught homiletics at Virginia Union for many years, was the catechizer who guided me through the process of ordination. According to Ellison, preaching is didactic reflection on the word. I was influenced by his book, *They Who Preach*. I have also been impressed and helped by many of the well-known and lesser-known pulpiteers in the black church; however, I am committed to my own style of delivery and exegesis, which I have developed over the past twenty years of serving as a pastor. The practice of preaching for me is always in process. Good preaching is a constant struggle.

The Preacher as Practical Intellectual

The black preacher, while not always formally educated, has historically been one who was well read and socially conscious to the extent that he or she could influence the community to mobilize its efforts towards liberation and transformation. Though not usually an academic, the preacher has been an intellectual. The preacher has systematically interpreted Scripture, history, and culture in a way that has expanded the understanding and perception of the church and community. The preacher has been willing and free to confront racism, discrimination, injustice, and unrighteousness in a way that no other black intellectual has been willing to risk. Many businesspeople, teachers, lawyers, and others have had their public speech muted by their private interests or some other fear of retribution by power brokers—clients, boards, public officials, and so on. Moreover, their constituency has often been limited and comparatively small when compared to that of the preacher, who often commands a large and loyal audience. The church and community have expected and even encouraged the preacher to speak out on issues that affect the freedom of the community. Most local communities can speak of heroes and leaders willing to speak about racism and injustice, and these heroes and leaders are often the local preacher.

Cornel West indicated that preaching and music have been institutionalized in the African American religious experience. They both are oriented toward the participation and development of community. In *Breaking Bread,* West states:

> I would suggest that there are two organic intellectual traditions in Afro-American life: the Black Christian tradition of preaching and the black musical tradition of performance. Both traditions, though undoubtedly linked to the life of the mind, are oral, improvisational, and histrionic. The richness, diversity, and vitality of the traditions of Black preaching and Black music stand in strong contrast to the paucity, even poverty, of Black literate intellectual production.[4]

West argues that although there have been some literate black intellectual giants, they do not compare with those who have been sustained by the church and the community. The preacher who has a church and a pulpit to speak from every Sunday has influence over the largest numbers of persons in the community, and because the church is so powerfully institutionalized the impact of the preacher is unquestionable. Moreover, because there are hundreds of churches in every city, the voice of the preacher is heard from every corner of the community, and this voice affects the beliefs and practices of an inordinate number of people. As an intellectual, the preacher is compelled to deal with issues that prick the soul and the conscience of society, issues of liberation and transformation as dictated by culture or life situation and by the biblical text. The explication of the text via the sermon is an intellectual project, and requires serious spiritual and emotional commitment to ministry as well as a thorough effort to engage the scriptural text in conversation with the real issues that face our communities. Violence, crime, education, poverty, morality, faith, fairness, justice, hope—must be addressed by the prophetic preacher.

On any given Sunday, one can hear a meaningful message being heralded from pulpits across the nation. Likewise, there can be heard a lot of hoopla, thunderous and boisterous sound that does not reflect the serious need to engage the biblical text and the congregation in a dialogue toward transformation and liberation. Ideally, every sermon should be a harbinger of liberation that germinates in the mind of the preacher and then radiates throughout the congregation, manifesting itself in renewed self-understanding and challenge to those who hear. Unfortunately, this is not always the case, and the preacher ends up conforming to existing norms within the congregation rather than transforming the listeners into new creations with the power of the preached word. The preacher has a responsibility to think through the word of God, to labor with the text, to wrestle with its meaning, its context, and its power to transform the life of the congregation and broader community. This demands intellectual rigor and integrity. The preacher as intellectual is not simply an intelligent person, but a thinker who practices and labors courageously with that which is thought, heralded, and explained. The preacher as intellectual is one who reads everything that she or he can get her or his hands on, from social philosophy and history to biblical theology, poetry, and autobiography. Moreover, the preacher needs to know about business and technology, current events and the economy. Ultimately, the preacher needs to have a wholistic view of the community and world. The preacher as intellectual is not caught up in what is popular and expedient, or what makes folk shout and holler, but is caught up in what is transformative, whether the hearer likes it or not. The preacher is not in a popularity contest! This means that he or she may or may not be well liked, but he or she is often well respected. Respect often obviates dislike and certainly compensates for it. The preacher is one who understands that the practice of ministry, and especially preaching, is a calling to transform and liberate the oppressed and the oppressor. The preacher as intellectual cannot conform either to the ways of the world or to the ways of the status quo church, because their ways are too similar and often too familiar. The preacher as intellectual is a bold prophet, a doer, a speaker of truth—no matter how bitter or confrontational, or unpopular that truth may be.

The preacher as intellectual does not revel in simply providing a cognitive or emotional escape from the realities of injustice, but forces the congregation to deal with the social environment and its effects on the poor or disenfranchised or those on the bottom of society. The preacher as intellectual is represented by persons such as the late Benjamin E. Mays, Mordecai Johnson, Joseph T. Hill, John Malcus Ellison, and Howard Thurman, as well as those working today—Renita J. Weems, Samuel D. Proctor, Gayraud S. Wilmore,

Miles Jones, Leontyn Kelley, Praithia Hall-Wynn, Samuel Roberts, Boykin Sanders, Jackie Grant, Charles Adams, Charles B. Copher, John W. Kinney, Robert L. Stephens, and a host of other well-known and lesser-known heralders of the gospel.

I believe the preacher is called to develop the sermon in a thorough and helpful way so that the church can make a difference in the lives of those who gather in her pews Sunday after Sunday and year after year to hear a word from the Lord! Preaching that is liberative and transformative is indeed indicative of the word that issues forth from the prophetic formula, "thus saith the Lord" (Jer. 2:5; 6:22; 7:20; Isaiah 1:24; 7:7; 43:1; Amos 1:3, 9; 2:1, 4, 6).

Textuality in Preaching

The biblical text was written to inspire faith and belief in God. Accordingly, preaching is distinguished from all other discourses in that the source for the discourse is other than the preacher, him or herself. In Christian proclamation the course is the scriptural or canonical text from the Old or New Testament—the inspired Word of God. The preacher's ability to deal faithfully and thoroughly with the scriptural text is a sine qua non to preaching. In my view, the textuality of the message determines its validity and establishes the message as an authentic sermon rather than a religious speech, a powerful oration, or a spiritual discourse. In its authentic form, the sermon is more than a powerful speech or a moving discourse because it is grounded in the scriptural text. Moreover, using of religious language in an oral discourse does not mean a sermon is being preached, because one can potentially miss the importance of the text. A sermon is more than eloquent speech or syncopated tonality melodiously massaging the ears and the heartstrings of the people. A sermon is wrestling with the biblical text in all of its nuances, character, history, and context in order to present a word from a higher source to seek to make sense out of confused and chaotic experience. The sermon should bring order out of chaos, comfort out of sorrow, life out of death. A sermon does what the writer of the Pentateuch claims in the Genesis account of creation—out of nothing comes something (Gen 1:1-31). The chaos was transformed into order. A sermon is born out of the struggle to allow the text to explode and resonate, first in the soul and consciousness of the preacher. This explosion becomes enlightening, explanatory, exhilarating and ultimately transformative to both the preacher and hearer.

Too often, we hear messages from the pulpit that portend to be sermons when in fact the preacher has only chosen a text as a pretext for preaching—a convenient verse that he or she can use to extract a topic, or, more often, attach a topic, without regard for the fact that the text is the controlling element in the ability of the sermon to be transformative. Discourse under the aegis of sermonic proclamation grounded in something other than the biblical text is more predicatory, that is, more related to preaching or akin to preaching than to the actual development of a sound textually based sermon. In fact, it is far from it. Additionally, a message that is grounded in something other than the biblical text, that is, in sociology, psychology, literature, history, philosophy, or even human experience, makes a weak claim to being a sermon. The phenomenon of textuality constitutes the essence of sermonic discourse. If we could use the analogy of the Genesis account once again, too often the sermon is on the chaotic side, that is, it focuses on that which is other than the transformative word.

For me, textual preaching—choosing a text and developing a subject based on the chosen text, and then proceeding to develop the text in all of its fluidity and complexity—and applying the text to context and experience is the most essential requirement for preaching. Of course, this assumes that the preacher is acutely aware of the fact that the text presents a particular dimension of life and references a higher power. Preaching is essentially a textual enterprise because the transformative power of the sermon is grounded in the biblical text, not in the topic. Too often, the preacher will choose a text not simply as a *pretext* but also as a *pretense* to the real development of the scriptural text. He or she will pretend to develop the text but will in fact develop the topic, which often is out of synchrony and harmony with the chosen text. In my view, the development of a topic is not indicative of liberation and transformative preaching and does not suggest the formation of a sermon. The sermon must be thoroughly textual in all of its implications, and what we refer to as points, or what David Buttrick and others call moves, must flow from the text itself and not simply from biblical literature or theology. This means that the preacher must develop a new appreciation for the scriptural text itself and not succumb to the lure of popular culture to circumvent the text with a topic. Moreover, the story, the experience, and the ideal in the text must become real, both to the preacher and the hearer.

1

Telling It Like It Is:
From Liberation to Transformation

And ye shall know the truth, and the truth shall make you free.
—John 8:32, KJV

Now after that John was put in prison, Jesus came into Galilee,
preaching the gospel of the kingdom of God, and saying, The
time is fulfilled, and the kingdom of God is at hand: repent ye,
and believe the gospel.
—Mark 1:14-15, KJV

What Is Liberation and Transformation Preaching?

Liberation preaching is preaching that is transformational. This
means that it is intended to effect change in the nature and structure
of persons and society. Moreover, transformation means that the
condition of one's mental and physical existence has been altered.
Paul says, in the Book of Romans, "Do not be conformed to this
world but be transformed by the renewal of your mind . . . " (Rom.
12:2). The idea of preaching as liberation, as transformation and
change is also captured in 2 Corinthians: ". . . where the Spirit of the
Lord is, there is freedom. And we all, with unveiled face, beholding
the glory of the Lord, are being changed into his likeness from one
degree of glory to another . . . " (2 Cor 3:17-18a). The classic scriptural text that speaks of preaching liberation is attributed to Jesus
himself by the writer of Luke's gospel: "The Spirit of the Lord is upon
me, because he has anointed me to bring good news to the poor. He
has sent me to proclaim release to the captives and recovery of sight
to the blind, to let the oppressed go free" (Luke 4:18, NRSV).

Liberation is a precondition of transformation. This means that

8

before one can actually change one's life situation one needs to be free to do so. The process of transformation begins with a new understanding of consciousness which requires a mental and spiritual transformation.

In order for an individual or a society to be liberated and, ultimately, transformed, that individual or group needs first to understand that liberation means that his or her thoughts and actions are not simply a reflection of the thoughts of others, but rather of the ability to think and do for oneself. Our beliefs and practices are too often shaped by television and technology, popular culture and popular religion, rather than by a deep sense of moral responsibility and biblical reflection. While liberation is the sine qua non of transformation, transformation itself requires a new consciousness and a new mentality. This means that our total awareness and the ability to interpret that awareness must be reflected in preaching. Too many of those to whom we preach seem to feel a sense of detachment and obliviousness to the gospel—a feeling that "this doesn't apply to me," that "I am comfortably situated in my own private world." There is a need for a transformation of consciousness on the part of the preacher and the hearer of the gospel. The preacher's task is to interpret scripture in order to restructure human consciousness. This is very much what Jesus did in his preaching and teaching. Accordingly, the ultimate goal of liberation preaching is to transform, that is, to bring about change in one's condition by confronting the causes of that condition. Now, this transformation or change has two major dimensions. The first dimension can be described as individual change. Preaching that focuses on individual transformation and the collective transformation of individuals can certainly be liberationist. This type of liberation preaching constituted much of what I heard growing up in rural Virginia and often hear today. This form of liberation preaching encourages blacks and the poor to participate in the system, to get an education, to get involved in the political process, and to do those things that will gradually help to change and transform society. Transformation is encouraged through participating in those institutions that are designed to make a difference. This kind of preaching also is encouraging and uplifting. In his book *Uplifting the Race: The Black Minister in the New South 1865–1902,* Dr. Edward L. Wheeler explains the phenomenon of uplift as accommodation and assimilation but not submission or acquiescence. In discussing the message of the preacher during the years immediately following the Civil War, he says, "Their very belief that a broken people could be uplifted was in a sense revolutionary, because it said that Blacks had the potential to live in the society as equals rather than subordinates."[1] This uplifting message was indeed a form of liberation preaching that continues to be heard in the black church. This kind of preaching is what I heard as a child at Union Grove Baptist Church and Shiloh Baptist Church in Chesterfield, Virginia. When I was baptized in 1963 at the age of eleven by Rev. George Polk, I wanted to be uplifted and encouraged, because our family was poor and the long rows of tobacco that we had to harvest seemed never to come to an end. The times were hard, and I cannot forget the revival meetings and Sunday services in these churches, where pastors like Moses Knott, George Polk, Harold Braxton, and Fred J. Boddie Sr. would preach about God and Jesus in a way that gave my brothers and sisters and me the hope and determination to "keep on keeping on." This preaching was not about systemic injustice and oppression, or the pandemic presence of racism and discrimination, but it was uplifting, encouraging, and ameliorative. It helped us to cope with the hard times, the rural poverty, and the other troubles that we faced as families and individuals growing up on a back road in Chesterfield County, Virginia. This kind of liberation preaching makes the hearer understand that his or her life situation does not have to remain as it is. This preaching helped me to believe that I could indeed finish high school and go on to college, although no one else in my family had done this before. This preaching was and is uplifting, and I believe Ed Wheeler describes not only the message of the preachers in the thirty-seven years following 1865 but through most of this century when he concludes that "accommodation and possibility then were inter-related aspects of what uplift was all about."[2] In this preaching, I heard possibility and hope, and to that extent, I heard liberation preaching.

The second dimension of liberation preaching is the transformation of society or of systems that often appear to absorb and nullify individual efforts. This preaching recognizes that assimilation often breeds co-optation, and, more important, it realizes that even the collective effort of individuals is often met with the sin and evil that are inherent in principalities and powers in society. This type of liberation preaching has given up on advocating that an increase in education or participating in the structures that are oppressive will somehow change the structure itself. This dimension of liberation as transformation reads the Bible with a specific interest in changing the nature and structure of society to alleviate poverty and injustice. For example, Jesus says in Luke's gospel: "I came to bring fire to the earth, and how I wish it were already kindled! . . . Do you think I have come to bring peace to the earth? No, I tell you, but rather division!" (Luke 12:49, 51, NRSV). Not only does Jesus utter radical statements such as this, but he is very concerned about issues of justice and the manifestation of love. He insults and castigates the Pharisees because of their interest in maintaining the status quo. He says "But woe to you Pharisees! For you tithe mint and rue and herbs of all kinds, and neglect *justice* and the *love* of God; it is these you ought to have practiced, without neglecting the others" (Luke 11:42, NRSV; emphasis added). Jesus was confronted constantly with the absence of justice in the attitudes and practices of the Pharisees and scribes. His own social context precipitated the often searing and terse statements he made to his antagonists, who sometimes were his own disciples. Preaching liberation means capturing the spirit of protest in the words of scripture and particularly in the message of Jesus and sharing that spirit with those who are oppressed as well as the oppressors. Leonardo and Clodovis Boff, two South American priests/theologians, capture the spirit of liberation preaching as transformation and change in discussing liberation hermeneutics.

> Liberation hermeneutics seeks to discover and activate the *transforming energy* of biblical texts. In the end, this is a question of finding an interpretation that will lead to individual change (conversion) and change in history (revolution). . . . For example, liberative hermeneutics will stress . . . the social context of oppression in which Jesus lived and the markedly political context of his death on the cross.[3]

Jesus is the most glaring example of the message of liberation, and the road he traveled ended in a cruel and debasing death. More precisely Jesus is the quintessential *Messenger* and embodied *message* of liberation. The ultimate expression of liberation is in the resurrection as symbol of newness, transformation, and change. Moreover, the resurrection is a symbol of victory and vindication, and in the black preaching tradition the resurrection event has historically been a clear component of the sermon.

Many preachers and theologians have sought to define and describe liberation theology in its many contexts and forms, from

Gustavo Gutiérrez, Leonardo and Clodovis Boff, and James H. Cone to Marc Ellis and Enrique Dussel.[4] However, after combing through these sources for their wisdom and insight, I must return to the one book that sustained me in this quest to understand the meaning of liberation preaching. This book, the Bible, has always been my source of strength and hope because within its pages are the transformative words of Jesus and the spirit and language of liberation and protest. I know there is much more in the Bible than the words of Jesus; however, it is in Jesus' words that a compelling and liberating motif emerges that lures and grips my soul and empowers me to preach the gospel.

In many ways transformation and liberation preaching is the forerunner of all Christian preaching because it is grounded in the message of Jesus. It is not confined to an understanding of theology that may be labeled "liberation theology." It is, however, preaching in the tradition of stalwarts of the faith and giants of the church such as Bishop Joseph Johnson, the Rev. Jerenna Lee, Vernon Johns, Mordecai Johnson, Martin Luther King Jr. These persons were proponents of "uplift," education, and transformation of both the individual and the system. Liberation preaching is preaching that challenges the established and prevailing social order, which is often the source of poverty, oppression, and injustice. However, liberation preaching has an even broader context, because persons come to church in order to get prepared to deal with the social order and they expect the preached word to assist in that preparation. Therefore, liberation preaching deals also with the liberation of the mind, body, and spirit. It enables blacks and whites to deal with racism, classism, and sexism as well as poverty and economic injustice by confronting these issues through actions that will bring about change.

Modern preachers such as Robert L. Stephens, pastor of Peace Baptist Church, Kansas City, Missouri; Mac Charles Jones, pastor of St. Stephen Baptist Church in Kansas City; Geoffrey Guns, pastor of Second Calvary Baptist Church, Norfolk, Virginia; and John Kinney, pastor of Ebenezer Baptist Church, Beaver Dam, Virginia, seem to embody the concept of liberation preaching as they seek to educate and empower people in the black community by doing what is necessary to develop housing, create jobs, and engender self-esteem. There are indeed other persons throughout this country who are equally progressive and committed to the liberation struggle.

Liberation preaching is preaching resistance to popular culture. Again, this is reflected in the life and message of Jesus (see Luke 4:18;

7:36-50), who seemingly did not care about being accepted by social elites or other religious leaders. In reference to Jesus' resistance, David Buttrick says, "because he was liberated, he did not have to belong . . . he was at liberty to be with the excluded because he never sought to be socially included."[5] Jesus resisted the co-optation of the status quo and preached resistance (see Mark 2:13-17, Matt. 21:12–17).

The preacher is a practical theologian, a proclaimer of the word. Certainly he or she is not usually a systematic or philosophical theologian, neither a church historian nor social ethicist, but one whose primary task is to preach whenever called upon. The words of James Cone, although meant for the theologian, also apply to the preacher. Cone says, "As preacher the theologian is a proclaimer of the Word, the truth of Jesus Christ as the Liberator of the poor and the wretched of the land. Here the theologian recognizes the *passionate* character of theological language. It is a language of celebration and joy that the freedom promised is already present in the community's struggle for liberation."[6] Likewise, the preacher recognizes the words of scripture and particularly the message of Jesus vis-à-vis our experience as the source of liberation preaching.

Preaching and the Language of Liberation and Prophecy

What we say is as important if not more important than how it is said. Preaching in the black tradition has generally focused on *how* and *what*. Because both *how* and *what* are important in the communication process, it is not my intent to juxtapose the two; however, at this juncture, I am mainly concerned with the what and not the how.

Language plays an important role in the preaching event and the struggle for liberation. If the preacher is to preach liberation and transformation then he or she will have to use language that conveys the idea and practice of freedom. His or her language has to be bold not timid and tepid. One cannot easily talk about freedom while using the language of oppression and injustice. Freedom has to be talked! It has to be preached, and the language has to make people feel that freedom is an end that can be achieved in our lifetime. Moreover, this language of freedom needs to be clear and precise in order to be rhetorically engaging and theologically sound.

The language of history, expressing the hopes and aspirations, sorrows and agonies, pain and suffering of a people whose quest for freedom seemed sometimes elusive, is nevertheless heard in one of the most free forms of expression in African American culture: the sermon. The language of liberation is found throughout the Bible, especially in the many Old Testament stories where we hear words of freedom, transformation, and liberation. From the pages of the Bible, the preacher can discover themes of freedom and liberation that need to be shared with the church and society as we endeavor to preach the gospel. James Cone, in *Speaking the Truth,* says that in the black tradition, preaching as prophecy essentially is telling God's story.

> "Telling the story" is the essence of black preaching. It means proclaiming with appropriate rhythm and passion the connection between the Bible and the history of black people. What has Scripture to do with our life in white society and the struggle to be *somebody* in it? To answer that question the preacher must be able to tell God's story so that the people will experience its liberating presence in their midst.[7]

African American preaching has traditionally related Scripture to the social condition of oppressed people and has been able to correlate this condition with the presence of sin and evil in the world. The preacher tells it like it is, believing that God has told him or her what to say and he or she is compelled to tell it to the congregation, because the truth can and does indeed set us free.

The preached language of liberation and transformation starts with the words of Jesus, whose language was radical and bold, often shocking those who listened. Joseph Johnson reminds us that "the radicalness of the humanity of Jesus is not only expressed in his service but also in his speech. We must permit his speech to address, probe, disturb, and challenge us."[8] In reading the Synoptic Gospels, we readily sense the liberation tone of the language that Jesus used. There was often a searing and "no-nonsense" response to the inquiries, doubts, and religious snobbery of the Pharisees and scribes. Johnson continues:

> The words of Jesus have the rugged fiber of a cypress tree and the jagged edge of a crosscut saw. His language is extreme, extravagant, explosive as hand grenades which are tossed into the crowds that listened to him. . . . He attacks the religious establishment of his day—the religious leaders, the ordained

ministers with such phrases as "you hypocrites," "you blind guides," "you blind Pharisees," "you brood of snakes," "you serpents," "you murderers."[9]

This tough language provides a model for preachers who endeavor to confront the status quo and the issues of injustice and oppression that pervade the church and social structure.

Preaching and the Kingdom of God

The preacher, like the theologian, is very much concerned about telling people about Jesus as the liberator and transformer of individuals and society in a way as passionate as Jesus' own. Preaching demands a passionate conviction about the proclaimed word, and I believe that the message of Jesus is intended to create a new worldview, that is, a new understanding of self and world in order that the kingdom of God may be closer to becoming a present reality.[10] Preaching liberation, then, is preaching about the kingdom of God, which is manifested, actualized, and fulfilled in Jesus (see Mark 1:15; Luke 4:21). In their book *Jesus and the Ethics of the Kingdom,* Bruce Chilton and J.I.H. McDonald say, "In Luke, this liberation motif is expounded with particular force (cf. 4:18f.). Jesus' proclamation and ministry signal the time of fulfillment: (4:21) the time when Scripture is fulfilled, the Kingdom actualized; . . . and when welcome news is given to the poor, release to the captives, sight to the blind and freedom to the oppressed."[11]

The kingdom of God, then, is about understanding liberation, because Jesus symbolizes the essence of the kingdom and preaching liberation is in effect preaching the kingdom of God, as Justo and Catherine Gonzalez say in *Liberation Preaching: The Pulpit and the Oppressed:*

> A theology of liberation is a theology of the Kingdom. The goal toward which we move is the fulfillment of the promises of the Kingdom. . . . Since in Christ the Kingdom has come, we can now live out of that new order. But since he is also still to come, we are not yet liberated, but in the process of being liberated. . . .[12]

Preachers, as bearers of the kingdom of God (see Luke 10:9-12), are indeed liberationist, because the kingdom of God represents a new social order as well as a new understanding of Scripture, which is a prerequisite to liberation homiletics. Moreover, because Jesus says that the kingdom of God is at hand in his own presence (Mark 1:15), those who preach the gospel are indeed bearers of the kingdom.

Preaching in Context

The African American church was born and raised on preaching. The desire to worship the Lord in a free and unencumbered manner was the driving force for the independence of most black churches. If this were not the case, many of us would still be sitting in the balcony or constituting the kitchen clubs in the white First and Second Baptist churches of the South. In this connection, the history of Second Baptist Church is an example of a black church being guided by its focus on preaching. Moreover, its withdrawal from the white church was by its very nature an act of defiance and liberation. Black folk did not want to continue under the dominant hand of whites, so they liberated themselves from the hypocrisy and oppressive rule of the white church. In this sense, the establishment of independent black churches was an act of resistance and liberation. This resistance reflects the African American people's unwillingness to believe that God intended that they be slaves, even in worship.

Preaching has been central to the life and history of the black church, and African American preachers did what was necessary to survive and to encourage the congregation in the midst of segregation, Jim Crow laws, and other forms of degradation and discrimination. It seems that there was little systematic effort to address homiletically the systemic ills that plagued African Americans and poor people. Their preaching, however, was liberationist to the extent that it focused on integration, uplift, and education, but not to the point of advocating a new social order or a new kingdom in the radical and transformative sense that Jesus represented and proclaimed.

The Liberating and Transformative Message of Jesus

> Now after John was arrested, Jesus came into Galilee, preaching the gospel of [the kingdom of] God, and saying, "The time is fulfilled, and the kingdom of God is at hand; repent, and believe in the gospel." (Mark 1:14–15, RSV alt.)

Today there are many messages being circulated, advocated, and promulgated. Everywhere we turn a message is being conveyed to us, through the media or some other means of making things known. Everywhere we turn somebody is sharing a message. Messages are covert and overt, intended and unintended, subtle and explicit, dramatic and undramatic; messages are written and unwritten, spoken and unspoken. Messages take different forms, are stated in different ways, and have different goals. They are clear and unclear, subtle and blatant. Some messages are urgent and demand an urgent response; other messages do not require a response. Messages are also meant for particular readers or hearers. For example, when I was a youngster in elementary school, I remember sending messages across the classroom writing notes, being careful that the teacher never saw me. Many others have undoubtedly done the same thing. We send messages in different ways. Sometimes, the way we act conveys a message. The way we look, talk, walk, smile, frown, complain, or even the way we dress conveys a message. Television is a message-maker, a modern means of making a major impact upon the minds of men and women, children, and youth. When our children see violence and hate, when they see horror and fear, guns and knives and decapitated bodies, drugs and easy money on television, we fail to realize that a message is being taped by their brain and recorded in their memory—a message that can come back automatically to haunt them and us at any time. The receiver has only to press the "rewind button" in his memory and this unconscious message becomes conscious again. This hidden, latent, dormant, subconscious, message resurfaces. I recently heard a preacher share a news story about a group of boys who were acting out the message they had learned from movies and television. I believe the incident took place in Boston. A group of boys were walking in a secluded area and saw a young black mother walking in the same secluded vicinity. They decided on a whim to "act out" some of these evil, sinful, and horrifying messages they had received from the television and movies. They raped this young woman, beat her, and stabbed her as she pleaded for her life. The autopsy showed that she had multiple stab wounds, any one of which was deep enough to kill her. They killed that young woman many times. When asked why they would do something so heinous, so horrible, so evil and sick, one young man replied that they simply "wanted to have some fun, to do something to act out a fantasy." Messages are critically important today, and we

need to be careful about the messages that we send with our attitudes and actions, our words and deeds, with the way we live, what
we say to others and what we don't say, what we write on paper or
whisper to our friends. Yes, there are all kinds of messages being
transmitted and disseminated, but there is only one message that
can transform us and the entire social structure. There are all kinds
of messages, but *the message* that the black church needs to hear and
to heed is not the message of the media. It is not the message of
movies or billboards. This message is not the message of rap, or reg-
gae, not the message of rhythm and rhyme, blues and bop, pop or
soul—it is not even the message of any music or melody. No, there
is only one basic, essential, transforming, liberating message that
has power in season and out of season, that can convince, convict,
convert, rebuke, rekindle and revive, teach and inspire, one message
that can console and comfort, that can heal and help persons who
are poor and distressed. This message is the message of Jesus Christ.
Jesus is the essence of the gospel message. This message is the
preaching of the gospel. Jesus didn't come after John inquiring
about a consensus of beliefs or taking an opinion poll in order to tell
folk what they wanted to hear or reinforce what they had already
heard. No! Jesus didn't come "shucking and jiving," not even praying and singing. He didn't come with a band of angels, an angelic
chorus, or an army of soldiers. He came without props and pretense,
without form or fashion, without "ifs" and "buts"—with nothing to
make him popular or even accepted by the religious authorities and
political leaders. No, Jesus came not wedded to the past of Jewish
tradition and custom, nor did he come promising a blissful future.
He simply came "preaching the gospel of [the kingdom] of God"
(Mark 1:14, RSV alt.) He came with a message—a message from
God and the power of the Holy Spirit. It was not a flowery message,
and it did not titillate the ears or massage the egos of the power
elites. It was not a message laced with pretty words or empty phrases.
It certainly was not what the scribes, Pharisees, or Herodians wanted
to hear! It was not a message that reinforced tradition or soothed the
conscience. But it was a liberation message, a message of transformation that needed to be heard and heeded by kings and princes,
young and old, rich and poor. It needed to be heard by all who
sought to understand that the kingdom of God is manifested in
Jesus Christ. It was a message that needed to be heard in Greece and
Rome, in Galilee and Galatia, in Judea and Samaria, in Palestine and
Syria, in Egypt and Jerusalem. This same message needs to be heard

by all who seek to be children of the living God. Well, what is the message of Jesus for the church today? What was the nature of Jesus' preaching? What does the message of Jesus have to say to us about preaching liberation?

First, we are compelled to recognize that the kingdom of God is already upon us. It is time for the power and presence of God to reign over us. In this text, we note that John had already prepared the way for Jesus, and now Jesus is present in the flesh. The preparation had been done and Jesus arrives preaching that "the kingdom of God is at hand." Some of the people, no doubt, were still looking for a kingdom represented by the posh and glitter of a king. The "king" and the kingdom cannot be separated, but the kingdom of God as manifested in Jesus Christ is a revolutionary and new phenomenon that alters one's understanding and actions—yes, this is the kingdom of God as realized in the person and teachings of Jesus. This text tells us that the kingdom has come in Jesus and it is at hand right now. And, if we are to be a part of the kingdom of God, receiving the ministry of Jesus Christ as a gift from God, we have to be obedient to the will of God. The kingdom of God is not *our kingdom,* where we rule and control; the kingdom of God is, for example, a far cry from some of our auxiliaries and groups in the church, where we have established our own kingdoms for many, many years. No, we have confused the kingdom of God with another kingdom. Jesus tells us about this kingdom in the Gospel according to Matthew:

> "Think not that I have come to abolish the law and the prophets; I have come not to abolish them but to fulfill them. . . . Whoever then relaxes one of the least of these commandments and teaches men so, shall be called least in the kingdom of heaven, but he who does them and teaches them shall be called great in the kingdom of heaven. For I tell you, unless your righteousness exceeds that of the scribes and pharisees, you will never enter the kingdom of heaven" (Matt 5:17, 19–20 RSV; emphasis added).

The kingdom of God requires some sacrifice and discipline. We are to first seek the kingdom of God and all other things will be added unto us. This means that we must make the life of Jesus our life, we must make his message our message. We must practice the teachings of Jesus with new commitment and a new determination to do justice. In the kingdom of God that is present in Jesus, there is not only peace and love, but there is a new meaning to these virtues. There is unity and community, there is justice and righteousness, there is obedience and sacrifice, there is discipline of mind and body. In the kingdom of God there is receptivity to the liberating and redeeming word of God, because in the word there is power to understand his kingdom: "The time is fulfilled and the Kingdom of God is at hand" (Mark 1:15a). Participation in the kingdom of God means participating in the liberating power of the teachings of Jesus as manifested in his words and deeds.

Finally, the message of Jesus is one of transformation and faith. He simply said "repent ye, and believe the gospel" (Mark 1:15b, KJV). Notice the order: "repent ye, and believe the gospel." To repent suggests that we have to turn from sin and evil and turn to the Lord. It also means that we must change directions, or change course. It means that we are to change attitudes, change hearts, change our focus, our traditional thoughts, change our understanding, our perspective, change our practices and the way we understand our relationship to others. Repent! When we turn from something and turn to Jesus, that indicates change. The kingdom of God is about *change!* The message of Jesus is about change! It demands a change in our worldview, in our understanding and actions. The word of God calls and causes us to change. If we think today that we can hear the message of Jesus and not be transformed, there is something fundamentally wrong with our understanding of the gospel. The gospel, the message of Jesus, is about the process of folk changing their ways, changing direction, changing their practices, changing their habits. Jesus came preaching repentance and belief. Yes, the gospel, the good news about the kingdom of God, can indeed change us. This good news is transformational. It can change the way we talk, it can change the way we live, it can change the way we treat one another. Yes, Jesus has a new message and he is that message. Yes, Jesus has a new message: "You have heard that it was said to the men of old, 'You shall not kill; and whoever kills shall be liable to judgment. But I say to you that every one who is angry with his brother shall be liable to judgment . . . and whoever says, 'you fool!' shall be liable to the hell of fire" (Matt 5:21). Jesus has a new message: "You have heard that it was said, 'You shall not commit adultery.' But I say to you that every one who looks at a woman lustfully has already committed adultery . . . in his heart" (vv. 27, 28). "If your right eye causes you to sin, pluck it out and throw it away; it is better that you lose one of your members than that your whole body be thrown into hell" (v. 29). "You have heard that it was said, 'You shall love your neighbor and hate your enemy.' But I say to you, 'Love your enemies and pray for those who persecute you, so that you may be sons of your Father who is in heaven; for he makes his sun rise on the evil and on the good and sends rain on the just and on the unjust'" (vv. 43–45).

The message of Jesus is a message about change; it is a message about personal and societal transformation. One can't authentically hear the gospel and not change. The gospel demands it! Oh, it's a message of repentance and belief. Anyone who truly encounters the gospel cannot be the same. There will be a difference in the way you see yourself; there will be a difference in your treatment of your brother or your sister. When you encounter the transforming power of the gospel, your entire world has changed because Jesus represents newness and change; he represents transformation and liberation!

The Centrality of Theology in Preaching

> I feel like a child of God this morning.
> —William H. Pipes, *Say Amen, Brother!*

The black preacher has traditionally known that God is a God of justice, ultimately concerned with the freedom of the oppressed. Moreover, whether he preached survivalism, integration, separation, or transformation, the preacher grounded his perspective in the word of God. In the Bible, God is "all in all," the "I am that I am." God is Father, Son, and Holy Spirit, possessing all divine attributes.

Certainly, the God of history is not limited to the experience of Abraham, Isaac, and Jacob. The concept of God as a focal point for reverence and worship is inherent in all religions. For example, we know that the Babylonians' God was Marduk, who acquired the status that Zeus would later hold in the Greek parthenon. For Socrates, that teacher of teachers, known as a gadfly, God was to be obeyed. Upon being indicted by the men of Athens for corrupting the youth and being accused by Miletus of being an atheist, he says: "Men of Athens, I honor you and love you; but I shall obey God rather than you."[13] This sounds much like Paul's language in the Acts of the Apostles when he stood in the midst of Mars Hill and said, "Ye men of Athens, I perceive that in all things ye are too superstitious. For as I passed by, and beheld your devotions, I found an altar with this inscription, 'To the unknown God.' Whom therefore you ignorantly worship, him I declare unto you. God that made the world and all things therein, seeing that he is Lord of heaven and earth, dwelleth not in temples made with hands . . . For in him we live, and move and have our being. . ." (Acts 17:22ff, KJV). The black church believes Scripture when it records, "Hear, O Israel; the Lord Jehovah our God [Elohim] is one Lord (Deut. 6:4), or "The fool hath said in his heart, There is no God." (Ps. 53:1, KJV).

Although the Western church has often talked about God in many wonderful and alluring ways, it historically has not thought of God as a friend to those who are the object of sneers and jokes and of the victims of systematic oppression and injustice. God has taken on the features of those who wrote about God's nature, and the attributes of God's power often reflect the power of those doing the writing. Therefore, when blacks began to write about God, some of the myths about the nature and character of God began to be corrected, and God became a part of our experience.

Preaching about the power of God in the life and history of the black church experience is sine qua non to action and reflection. The preacher's ability to have a word from the Lord to share with the community of faith is indicative of the power of God at work in the life of the heralder of the good news as well as those who come to hear a word of comfort. The black preacher, through his or her communicative skills and the help of the Holy Spirit, is able to help the congregation experience the meaning and power of God. In the act of preaching, God is truth and spirit, and we worship God in spirit and truth.

To the black preacher and to those who live in poverty and in the constant presence of humiliation and degradation, God is not confined to classical arguments about cosmology and metaphysics. God is not limited to the traditional understanding of history and theology. God is both friend and comforter. God is the one who troubles the waters of hatred, injustice, and oppression. Few can describe God with the eloquence and imagination of the preacher. The preacher is able to talk of God in terms that engender faith and fear, strength and power. When the preacher speaks of God, people cry and shout, weep and moan, believing that God is able to do all things —even to liberate people from sin and oppression.

God and Human Experience: How I Got Over

My understanding of God began to take shape during the early years of my life in the "house church" services we had growing up in central Virginia. We lived a rather isolated life, inasmuch as all of our neighbors on one side of the road were relatives. However, on the other side of the road was a very well-to-do white family who had sharecroppers tending their land. I observed very early that there was a striking contrast between the way we lived and the way that whites directly across the road from us lived. This family and their geographical proximity to us represented a glaring contrast between the social and economic conditions of blacks and whites. I often wondered why was this the case. Was there justice in any of this? Although these questions lingered in my mind, I would find comfort in the words of the Psalmist—words that I read and memorized at an early age:

> O Lord, how many are my foes!
> Many are rising against me;
> many are saying to me,
> "There is no help for you in God."
>
> But you, O Lord, are a shield around me,
> my glory, and the one who lifts up my head.
> I cry aloud to the Lord,
> and he answers me from his holy hill.
>
> I lie down and sleep;
> I wake again, for the Lord sustains me.
> —Ps 3:1-5, NRSV

These words of complaint and trust characterized my relationship with God. I felt that God understood our social condition, and that he would sustain us in the midst of doubt as we were growing up on "the place" as we often called the area where we lived.

My father was poor, a hard worker who labored tirelessly in order that his ten children and other relatives (nieces and nephews) would have something to eat and meager clothes to wear. As a child, I feared the death of my parents and would often pray that God would protect them. I knew then that I could not cope with such a loss and, as time passed, I began to focus on other things. In retrospect, I am convinced that had my mother or father died when I was much younger, I would have been devastated. I mention this because my family was such an intimate part of my life and my understanding of God. God was the protector who, in the language of the church, "made a way out of no way."

My very being was deeply interwoven with their existence and well-being. I believe that we were so close because of our rural location and because we often spent time singing and praying together. As a matter of fact, even today, when my parents and grandparents are dead and gone, their memory will always be with me. So I cannot reflect upon God without thinking about my background and remembering the nexus that existed between my parents, my brothers and sisters, and myself, and without believing that God indeed has been "a shield around me, my glory, and the one who lifts up my head" (Ps 3:3). We were such a close-knit group growing up in rural poverty that I was almost totally unaware of how poor we really were. I often wonder why we felt so at ease, so protected and fearless. Now I know that God blessed us to have both parents and the company of one another, not to mention other cousins, aunts, and uncles. We were a family in the best sense of the word. We were not a nuclear family in the traditional, sociological sense because we were more than that—we were well extended.

I remember the early years when we all lived near my grandmother's house. We called it the "big house" because it was big enough for all of us to gather for prayer meetings, sing praises, and hear sermons by my uncles and sometimes by a white, "jack-leg" preacher, as he was often called. I do not know why he was preaching to us in our family's central meeting place except that he was a friend to one of my uncles. I remember distinctly that preaching and singing took place long before I ever went to an organized church. My father used to talk of being a preacher, and people would say, "He would make a good preacher," but he never felt the call to preach. Those early experiences of praising God in my grandmother's house help to shape my view of God. I was frustrated with the social conditions, but I was never without hope, because I believed that God was real and powerful. However, my understanding of God was strengthened and further developed during my seminary days when Mac Charles Jones, Robert Stephens, and I would discuss theology and James Cone's *God of the Oppressed* and J. Deotis Roberts' *A Black Political Theology.* These works had a significant effect on my understanding of God from a black liberation perspective.

God Is Liberator

In transformation preaching one understands God as the liberator. God's power and God's love are all meshed into a supreme entity who has the power to set at liberty those who are downtrodden and oppressed. Warren Stewart Sr., a pastor and author, suggests that the liberating power of God is for everyone. The oppressors are also oppressed and need to be liberated from the will to dominate others. Stewart says:

> However, this liberating quality of God does imply that every person or group that professes to believe in the God of the Christian faith must recognize the need for liberation whether on a personal, social, or communal level. This can only be done through the process of continuous self-examination and interaction with members of the oppressed as well as the oppressors. God must be approached as a liberator by us who are bound by our cultural differences, acquired prejudices, handed-down traditions, and propensity toward homogeneity. Each of us who is assigned to interpret the Word of God . . . must first be liberated by the God of liberation."[14]

In our preaching we can indeed tell the truth of Scripture and tradition, which is an act of liberation in itself. We are compelled to share with people through our preaching the various biblical stories that speak of God as freedom-giver, and then relate these stories to the past and present experience and condition of African Americans. For example, the Book of Exodus begins with Israel's bondage in Egypt; however, in spite of the oppression that the Israelites experienced, God through his servant Moses led them from bondage to freedom.

Black people can identify with God as liberator because stories such as this perfectly correlate with the experience of slavery in American history and the liberating power of God in the process of emancipation (see Exod 1:1ff.) James Weldon Johnson, novelist, poet, linguist, and educator, captures the understanding of God as liberator in his classic book of sermons, *God's Trombones*. The sermon "Let My People Go" captures the liberating power and spirit of God as well as God's relationship to the oppressed.

> And God said to Moses:
> I've seen the awful suffering
> Of my people down in Egypt.
> I've watched their hard oppressors,
> Their overseers and drivers;
> The groans of my people have filled my ears
> And I can't stand it no longer;
> So I'm come down to deliver them
> Out of the land of Egypt,

> And I will bring them out of that land
> Into the land of Canaan;
> Therefore, Moses, go down,
> Go down into Egypt,
> And tell Old Pharaoh
> To let my people go.[15]

Preaching liberation and transformation means understanding God as Moses did, and trusting that God will indeed enable and empower us to speak the truth about the trials and tribulations of our own people to whoever needs to hear it. It means that the preacher will not be intimidated by the pharaohs of this world, but will know that God is a liberator for African Americans just as he was for the Hebrews. This same idea of God as liberator is found in Benjamin E. Mays' work *The Negro's God*. Mays quotes from a sermon titled "God Liberates Human Personality," in which the preacher clearly proclaims that God has the power to transform individuals and the social order. The following words indicate that God is a revolutionary change-agent who is able to effect change in the systemic ills of society. Mays states:

> Many are the human souls in this world with the capacity for the expression of the abundant life, if only the stone of remorse could be rolled away from the doorway of their hearts. Others there are whose lives would be gems of abiding influence if the stone of conceit could be rolled away. Whole communities could be electrified, changed, transformed if stones of shallowness, indifference, indolence, could be rolled back, so that the entombed life might come forth with glorified power and revolutionize the social order. . . . This rolling back of human repressions is absolutely essential to the peace and happiness of the world.[16]

God is not only the liberator, God is also mysterious. God's nature is such that the preacher knows only that God is God, and humankind cannot know all there is to know about God. No one, not even the great philosophers who claim to know more about the nature of God than anyone else, can fully discern the mysteries of God. In his book *Say Amen, Brother!* William Pipes reminds us of this through sermons presented in a style he identifies as "old-time Negro preaching." He quotes from the preacher's sermon titled "God's Mysteries upon the Mountains":

"There are so many men—some our great philosophers—have tried to dig out all the mysteries of God. Gone off to school and studied and all lika [sic] that, but there haven't been no man able to—to—to learn all the mysteries of God. Past man's finding out. So high, can't go over; so deep, can't go under; so wide, can't go around."[17]

God is not limited to our understanding or the lack thereof. All the mysteries of God have never been recorded. This is why the preacher believes that God cannot be circumscribed. Indeed, we cannot "get around" God as the omnipresent, mysterious liberator and as the God of love and justice.

Preaching and Christology: Jesus and the Church

In order to preach the gospel, the preacher needs to have a clear understanding of Christology, that is, probing the nature and meaning of Jesus for the church today. For the Christian, faith in Jesus Christ as redeemer and savior is the glue that holds the church together as a community of believers. In a time of troubling apathy, coupled with spiritual and social malaise in the church and society, the meaning of Jesus Christ gains new relevance. Jesus has historically held a sacred place in the life of the black Christian church. In the black preaching tradition, there has been a high Christology that places Jesus at the nucleus of worship and proclamation. "Jesus" and "God" are often used interchangeably, and in some instances I have observed that the church has acted as if Jesus were fully God altogether! I know that this may sound strange to some, but because there seems to be a prevailing high Christology at work, the humanity of Jesus is not something that the black church spends a lot of time contemplating, other than through focus on the cross and its role in the suffering of Jesus. The preacher often places little emphasis on the "fully human" characteristics of Jesus. The emphasis is on Jesus as "fully God." So, I believe it is fair to say that often in the black church community, Jesus is indeed God! There is an interchangeability between the use of the word "God" and "Jesus." This is evident in Zora Neale Hurston's poetic exposition, "The Sermon," based on an actual sermon she heard in which the preacher, in talking about the wounds of Jesus, constantly intones "God A'mighty," implying that Jesus is God Almighty.

"I can see Him step out upon the rim bones of
    nothing
Crying I am de way
De truth and de light.
Ah!
God A'mighty!
I see Him grab de throttle
Of de well ordered train of mercy
I see kingdoms crush and crumble
Whilst de angels held de winds in de corner
    chambers
I see Him arrive on His earth.
And walk de streets thirty and three years
Oh-h-hhh!
I see Him walking beside de sea of Galilee wid his
    disciples This declaration gendered on His lips
Let us go on to the other side
God A'mighty! . . ."[18]

During the time that Jesus walked the face of the earth, this question was debated by the disciples of Jesus as well as by his antagonists. Persons wondered both secretly and aloud about who this man
was. Jesus was later described by the early church as both human and
divine—fully God and fully man. This was a belief with which the
Docetists had severe difficulty, because they could not accept the
humanity of Jesus Christ. "Docetists were an obscure section of the
great Gnostic heresy. They taught that the body in which our Lord
suffered was not properly his own; that he had, indeed, no proper
manhood, and that he died only in appearance upon the cross."[19]
This theological belief was debated at the Council of Nicaea in 325,
and was defeated at the Council of Chalcedon because it had been
rejected by leaders of the day such as Clement of Alexandria and Ter-
tullian.[20] Nevertheless, "at the level of imagination, docetism is still a
common way of picturing Jesus as a divine being."[21] In this rather
positive sense, the black church and its preachers, who are masters of
imagination and hyperbole, could be described as somewhat docetic.
The "fully God" status of Jesus makes Jesus "Almighty," that is, able
to do what God does. This view of the omnipotent God is then trans-
ferred to Jesus. But, unlike church history and philosophy, the words
of scripture make clear the nature of Jesus Christ:

> Have this mind among yourselves, which is yours in Christ Jesus, who, though he was in the form of God, did not count equality with God a thing to be grasped, but emptied himself, taking the form of a servant, being born in the likeness of men. And being found in human form he humbled himself and became obedient unto death, even death on a cross. Therefore God has highly exalted him and bestowed on him the name which is above every name, that at the name of Jesus every knee should bow, in heaven and on earth and under the earth, and every tongue confess that Jesus Christ is Lord, to the glory of God the Father (Phil 2:5-11).

The Logos and the suffering human being are indeed united in the preceding text, and I am sure that scriptures like this helped to defeat this doctrinal heresy as well as others.

Jesus is indeed man—born of a virgin of low estate (Luke 1:48). Scripture again states: ". . . the Angel Gabriel was sent from God to a city of Galilee named Nazareth, to a virgin betrothed to a man whose name was Joseph, of the house of David; and the virgin's name was Mary" (Luke 1:26-27). However, in his humanity, he was without sin. As a matter of fact, Jesus came forgiving sin and promising eternal life for those who believed. This posture and action caused friction between Jesus and many of the religious and political leaders of that day. So, who is Jesus Christ? He is Counselor, Comforter, Prince of Peace. To the Christian believer, he is the Messiah, the Savior. But, he is also one who upset the authorities by being in sharp and constant conflict with the priestly Saducean hierarchy in the temple. Jesus was a transformer of individuals and society. The Pharisees made it their business to question his authority constantly; nevertheless, he preached a message of freedom and transformation to those who ventured to listen. For example, his first sermon, according to the gospel writer Luke, was to reiterate the work that had been prophesied generations before: "The Spirit of the Lord is upon me, because he has anointed me to preach good news to the poor. . . . those who are oppressed" (Luke 4:18). Jesus was a preacher of the gospel truth. Through parables, stories, and illustrations from the experiences of the people, Jesus taught his disciples and others the meaning of justice and fairness, truth and love. Accordingly, he advocated change and transformation in the heart and in our actions. Jesus was one who, as Martin Hengel says, dared to "speak in God's stead."[22]

Jesus also fellowshipped with the poor, the outcasts. He made friends with the most unlikely segment of society, that is, persons whom others despised and ignored. He spent time with the lowly and was equally comfortable with the ungodly, those who one writer has called "the pariahs of Jewish society." Jesus also was a friend to tax collectors and sinners—those who were outwardly blameworthy and guilty of some of the things about which, even today, we whisper and gossip. When one encounters Jesus, or experiences his power, it is akin to nothing we have seen or heard before. Jesus has the power to change our worldview, the way we see ourselves in relation to others and the community. Jesus is indeed the catalyst for both internal change and external transformation.

Who is Jesus Christ? He tells us who he is through his message—a message that we need to hear and practice. As Jesus begins his activity in Galilee, he says:

> You have heard that it was said to the men of old, "You shall not kill; and whoever kills shall be liable to judgment; whoever insults his brother shall be liable to the hell of fire" . . . You have heard that it was said, "You shall not commit adultery," but I say to you that every one who looks at a woman lustfully has already committed adultery with her in his heart. . . . It was also said, "Whoever divorces his wife . . . except for the woman commits adultery. . . . You have heard that it was said . . . "You shall not swear falsely" . . . But I say . . . Do not swear at all . . . you have heard that it was said, "You shall love your neighbor and hate your enemy." But I say to you, Love your enemies and pray for those who persecute you . . . for [God] makes his sun rise on the evil and on the good, and sends rain on the just and on the unjust" (Matt 5:21ff.).

Jesus, the Liberator and Transformer

Black theology has described Jesus as the liberator, taking its cue from the words attributed to Jesus in Luke's gospel: "The Spirit of the Lord is upon me, because he has anointed me to preach good news to the poor . . . to set at liberty those who are oppressed, to proclaim the acceptable year of the Lord" (Luke 4:18). In this text, Jesus is seen as the ground of liberation. James Cone says, "Jesus Christ, therefore, in his humanity and divinity is the point of departure for . . . the meaning of liberation."[23] When we begin with Jesus as the liberator or the foundation upon which personal and societal transformation takes place, then we can do liberation preaching by reflecting upon the dimensions of Jesus Christ as liberator. This means that liberation and transformation preaching is kerygmatic preaching, as Bishop Joseph A. Johnson Jr. in his book *The Soul of the Black Preacher* explains:

> Jesus is liberator. He is the revelation of the wisdom, the power and the love of God. This was the message which the early Christian preachers were commissioned to proclaim. This message was called the kerygma. We preach Christ, Paul shouts. At the heart of the kerygma lies this fundamental christological affirmation: Jesus is the Liberator![24]

Indeed, the preacher is called to understand Jesus as one who lived and suffered the injustices of hate and even death on the cross. The black preacher has historically understood the way Jesus was treated as an example of unmerited suffering, and identified the suffering of black people during the periods of slavery, Jim Crowism, and covert racism with the suffering of Jesus. Zora Neale Hurston, an American prose writer, anthropologist, and member of the Harlem Renaissance, records a sermon she heard in 1929 in her book *The Sanctified Church*. The preacher in that text speaks of the suffering of Jesus.

> "I can see Him wid de eye of faith—
> When He went from Pilates house—
> Wid the crown of 72 wounds upon His head.
> I can see Him as He mounted Calvary and hung
>   upon de cross for our sins.
> And about dat time De angel of Justice
>   unsheathed
> his flamin sword and ripped de veil of de temple
> And de High Priest vacated his office. . . ."[25]

The view of Jesus as liberator and transformer does not deny his suffering, because black people are keenly aware of Jesus' suffering as well as their own. Jesus' power to overcome the suffering of the cross via the resurrection is the basis for Christian faith and hope. This is the faith that has sustained blacks from slavery to the present crisis among black males, whose specific condition will be dealt with in a later chapter. The resurrection is the most powerful symbol of liberation because it implies transformation and change in the most comprehensive and enduring way possible. It is in the resurrection story that the message of liberation is fully apprehended. Jesus overcomes death, hell, and the grave via the resurrection and establishes his victory over the power of sin and evil.

Who Is the Holy Spirit according to Scripture?

Who is the Holy Spirit and how does he help us? is an important question for the preacher in the black church. The preacher and the spirit are thought to be partners in the propagation of the gospel. The Spirit is that intangible force that hovers within and around us to encourage our desire to keep pressing on. The Holy Spirit is the power that dwells deep within our hearts that calls us to higher heights. The spirit is the breath of God within us. It is the urging, luring presence of God that enables us to do his will. The spirit was in Jesus when he began to preach in the temple, saying: "The Spirit of the Lord is upon me, because he has anointed me to preach good news . . ." (Luke 4:18). Paul points out that "the law of the Spirit of life in Christ Jesus has set me free from the law of sin and death" (Rom 8:2). In the spirit, there is life and peace, not the discord, divisiveness, and disunity that often plague the church.

In the Old Testament, spirit basically meant the breath of God or wind—"The spirit of God was moving over the face of the waters" (Gen 1:2). Something of this sort survives in Jesus' words when he says to Nicodemus, "The wind blows where it wills, and you hear the sound of it, but you do not know whence it comes or whither it goes; so it is with every one who is born of the spirit" (John 3:8). Paul, in preaching to the Romans, had reached the point in his ministry where he had grown strong in Christ. His message to the Romans reflects his own experiences of Jesus Christ. For many years, Paul had been engaged in missionary activities that were often difficult. He had encountered opposition, stumbling blocks; but most of all, he had experienced a great deal of stress and agony that made him tired and weak. In spite of this, he continued to rely on the power of the Holy Spirit, saying: "Likewise the Spirit helps us in our weakness" (Rom. 8:26). The moment of weakness is not discriminating because the strength of our bodies fades away like chronological time or like the grass and like the flower. We know that our strength shall not always be as it has been in the past; but when the vigor of our body and soul has to give itself up to weakness, the Holy Spirit reigns in the midst of our weakness. Indeed, the spirit was with Paul while he was being persecuted. When the Israelites' faith was being restored, God spoke to them saying, "Fear not, for I am with you, be not dismayed, for I am your God; I will strengthen you, I will help you, I will uphold you with my victorious right hand" (Isa 41:10). So, because we know that God has the power to change things, we also know that the spirit enables the power of God to reign in our hearts and lift us out of our agony—whether it's anger, hatred, mental or physical illness, the spirit of God does indeed help us.

To be in Christ is to know the Holy Spirit, who is the actual presence of God in our lives and actions. Sometimes, we feel that we can see God and touch God, especially in the worship experience. His holy presence, when felt by us, is the spirit. The Holy Spirit enables us to walk in darkness and know that we are not alone. The spirit enables the man or woman who believes in him to know that God is omnipresent. This experience of feeling God in our midst is reflected in the etymology of some of our spirituals and gospel hymns. His presence, according to oral tradition, allowed our foreparents, when working in the cotton and tobacco fields, to stop in the middle of their work and look to the sky saying, "Over my head—I hear music in the air—there must be a God somewhere," or, "Every time I feel the Spirit, I will pray." His presence is felt in times when we need to be protected from the power of evil and death. When the agony of life has caused us to feel helpless, and it seems as if we are alone, our confidence in God is unceasing. His presence protects us like it protected the Psalmist who wrote, "The Lord is my shepherd, I shall not want. He leads me beside still waters; he restores my soul. Even though I walk through the valley of the shadow of death, I fear no evil; for thou art with me; thy rod and thy staff, they comfort me. . . (Ps 23:1, 2b, 3a, 4). The spirit of God is a fixed presence within us that can be both aroused and quelled by the ego. The spirit does not come and go as is often implied by the actions of the church.

The spirit is not only present with us, but helps us in our weakness. Paul says, "For we do not know how to pray as we ought, but the Spirit himself intercedes for us with sighs too deep for words" (Rom 8:26). Paul knew something about weakness and the luring power of sin and evil. He says, "When I want to do right, evil lies close at hand" (Rom 7:21). He understood that humankind is prone to do the opposite of good. When he was in prison and under siege, he could cope with the vicissitudes of life because the spirit of God was with him. He says to the Philippians that complaints serve no purpose when we are in Christ: "I know how to be abased, and I know how to abound; in any and all circumstances, I have learned the secret of facing plenty and hunger, abundance and want" (Phil 4:12). But he learned this not on his own, but through Jesus Christ. He knew, with faithful assurance, that the spirit would help him in weakness, and I am convinced that our weakness, whether physical, mental, or spiritual, can be remedied by the power of the Holy Spirit.

The preacher cannot preach without the Holy Spirit. Regardless of one's ability, strength, or study habits, the sermon is ultimately a product of the power of the Holy Spirit, which enables us to utter "what thus saith the Lord." After study, prayer, writing, singing, and doing everything else to prepare ourselves for the task of proclamation, our weakness prevents us from being totally ready to preach. However, when it is time to preach the gospel of Jesus Christ, "the spirit helps us in our weakness."

Preaching and the Holy Spirit

The scripture clearly suggests that there is a correlation between preaching and the Holy Spirit. After Jesus was baptized, "The Spirit descended upon him" (Mark 1:10ff.). In Luke's gospel, during Jesus' first sermon, Jesus proclaims that he is anointed by the power of the spirit as he speaks words of liberation to his hearers (Luke 4:18). The relationship of the Holy Spirit to preaching has its foundation in scripture (cf. Acts 10:36ff.) and becomes epitomized in the message of Jesus Christ.

Likewise, preaching in the black church tradition is a spiritual enterprise. The preacher is expected to be anointed by the power of the spirit before there is any attempt to preach the word. This notion is evident in a sermon titled "Why We Come to Church" in William H. Pipes' book, *Say Amen, Brother!* Pipes records the words of the preacher: "The Lord say, 'Open yer mouth and I'll speak fer you.' See what the Spirit gwine do. Tryin' to preach the Word of God. Pray His will be done."[26] The Holy Spirit is viewed as the source of the preacher's ability to deliver the sermon. In other written sermons, and in my own experience, it is not unusual to hear the preacher utter phrases such as "I feel the spirit now" or "Come, Holy Spirit"[27] as a part of the sermon itself. The Holy Spirit is indeed an integral part of the preaching process. James Cone indicates that there can be no preaching unless the preacher is called by the Holy Spirit.

> In order to separate the preached Word from ordinary human
> discourse and thereby connect it with prophecy, the black
> church emphasizes the role of the Spirit in preaching. No one
> is an authentic preacher in the black church tradition until he
> or she is called by the Spirit.[28]

Professor Cone is on target. Preaching in the black church tradition
is indeed dependent upon the Holy Spirit as the anointing power
that makes prophetic utterance possible. This is also seen in James
Baldwin's *The Amen Corner,* where the character Margaret, the pastor of the church, preaches and sings. In one of the songs, she sings:
"I got the Holy Spirit to help me run this race. I got the Holy Spirit,
it appointed my soul a place."[29]

The nexus between preaching and the Holy Spirit is clearly established in the black preaching tradition. However, James Forbes, pastor of Riverside Church in New York City, summarized the tradition
and its relationship to scripture in a comprehensive way:

> Jesus came preaching in the power of the Spirit. . . . The great
> prophets of Israel who came before Jesus also proclaimed,
> "Thus saith the Lord," as the Spirit moved them. They
> addressed their times out of a definite sense of divine
> appointment and empowerment. The Apostles, whom Jesus
> initiated into the continuing work of the kingdom, were told
> to expect the coming of the Spirit, in whose power they were
> to bear witness to Jesus. . . . To preach today in Jesus' name,
> and to do so with power, still requires the enabling presence of
> the Holy Spirit. [30]

The black church understands that the Bible is replete with references to the Holy Spirit and the process of proclaiming the word of
God. The power of the Holy Spirit makes the sermon come alive; it
gives the sermon form and substance and causes the words that may
be written or unwritten to connect with the lives of the brothers and
sisters in the pews. This power is so prevalent and integral to the
preaching of the gospel that Forbes makes a universal statement: "I
do not know a conscientious preacher anywhere who would claim to
preach without at least some acknowledgment of the aid of the Spirit,
even if the minister did not tend to speak of it in that way."[31]

The preacher needs all the power he or she can muster, and the aid
of the Holy Spirit is necessary to preach about the transformation of
individuals and society. The aid of the Holy Spirit is necessary to
confront the issues of injustice and oppression that plague people on

every level and in every community. Anyone who attempts to speak as Jesus spoke, confronting the wielders of power and seeking to extirpate evil and injustice from the religious, social, political, and economic fabric of society, must welcome the aid of the Holy Spirit!

Conclusion

The preacher needs to embrace a theology that will address injustice and oppression wherever it resides. Preaching that is transformative must be a result of our struggle to make sense of God, Jesus Christ, the Holy Spirit, and the prevailing presence of injustice and oppression. The preacher's effort to systematically develop sermons around the theme of liberation and freedom inherent in the biblical texts will constitute a liberation and transformation homiletic that is grounded in Scripture. There is enough in the Bible to enable the preacher to address issues of liberation without compromising the integrity of Scripture or the ability to interpret Scripture with newness and boldness.

I believe that the African American preacher historically has been a liberation and transformation preacher—using the word as a two-edged sword against sin and oppression. While the language of liberation may have been masked and cloaked in understanding and compassion, the driving force behind the preacher's ability to "say a word from the Lord" was the belief that God would right the wrongs perpetrated against those persons subjected to evils and injustices promulgated by the desire to dominate and subjugate other human beings.

2

Preaching out of Season: The Centrality of History and Culture in Preaching

Preach the word, be urgent in season and out of season...
—2 Tim. 4:2

... One may get the idea that some of the slaves did not want
freedom. This is not true. I have never seen one who
did not want to be free ...
—Booker T. Washington, *Up from Slavery*

Woe unto me if I do not preach the Gospel!
—1 Cor. 9:16

Preaching and worship are indeed the soul of the church. Quite frankly, preaching *is* the center of the traditional black church experience. It is up to the preacher to help teach and inspire folk with sound, meaningful preaching that will transform lives. Christians get excited about good preaching, and the black preacher is often a master at telling the biblical story in such a way that the church understands, appreciates, and responds.

I am suggesting that preaching Jesus Christ means preaching liberation and transformation. But this kind of preaching often has "out of season" status, because it is never easy or popular for the preacher or the hearer. It requires prophetic boldness and a willingness to risk telling the truth. Preaching about freedom and transformation confronts some of the basic spiritual and social issues of our times. This kind of preaching deals with poverty, fairness, justice, humility, and other social, economic, and moral problems that face the church and society. However, I believe that this is the method that Jesus used to confront the prevailing problems of his own time. In the language of Ernst Kasemann, Jesus Christ means freedom from social and political oppression and freedom from economic injustice. In other words, the authentic preaching of the gospel is inherently oriented toward individual and societal freedom. The good news is that God has enabled Jesus to show us, by example, the meaning of freedom and liberation. Jesus means that we can face head on the fact that we may be disinherited, disenfranchised, distressed, and discouraged, but we are not defeated and certainly not destroyed (see 2 Cor 4:8–9). I am increasingly strengthened by knowing that Jesus embodies the perfect paradigm for preaching liberation. In other words, Jesus' life and mission, as well as his message, form the core of preaching liberation. Accordingly, we need to look again at the words of Jesus and begin to confront the structure of injustice through preaching. This, it seems to me, is the essential message of the gospel. There are enough—indeed, too many—proponents of the status quo. This is why there is an urgent need for effective preaching that is truthful, indicting, confrontational, straightforward—a radically simple strategy that will be heard and acted upon rather than alienating—preaching that will challenge and transform the prevailing power structures that tend to oppress minorities, women, and the poor. Now, for some blacks, liberation means also freedom from a vitiating lifestyle, self-rejection, drug abuse, family violence, and a host of other afflictions that we must face. We acknowledge that all of our suffering is not at the hands of others. If we are to take liberation seriously, then we must understand that Jesus calls us to all sorts of liberation.

In this chapter, I will construct a model for preaching liberation and transformation that will have as its constitutive parts our African and slave heritage, the Bible, and the persistent manifestation of social, political, and economic oppression. These elements, when properly understood, provide the architectonic for developing a liberation homiletic.

Licensed by the Spirit: Slave Preaching

Recapturing the spirit of slave religion and developing what Molefi Kete Asante calls an "Afrocentric idea" will broaden the foundation for a liberation homiletic.[1] With no thoughts of the romantic, let me

suggest that blacks need to recapture the quest for freedom and liberation that preoccupied our slave foreparents. Slave preaching was
by nature an act of defiance and rebellion—a quest for freedom and
humanness.

The words of the following traditional slave song, "Oh, Freedom,"
expressed the heartfelt disdain that both preacher and layperson felt
about the institution of slavery. Additionally, the desire to be free
and the spirit of defying the prevailing social structure are equally
evident in these words of liberation chanted so often in the black
church:

> Oh, Freedom! Oh, Freedom!
> Oh, Freedom over me!
> And before I'd be a slave,
> I'll be buried in my grave,
> And go home to my Lord and be free.

Religion was the nucleus of slave culture, and at the center of religion was the slave preacher and his message of freedom—often subtle
and indirect, but always expressing a yearning to be free.[2] Lewis V.
Baldwin, author of *There Is a Balm in Gilead,* echoes the sentiment of
W.E.B. Du Bois when he says that the single most important figure
in the black Christian experience was the black preacher.[3] Many
scholars have suggested that the African American preacher was
sometimes radical and revolutionary, as evidenced by the best-
known insurrection in America's history, led by the Rev. Nat Turner
in 1831 in Southampton County, Virginia. However, more often
than not, the preacher was a pragmatic, politically conservative
leader because of the bondage of slavery. Nevertheless, freedom was
a basic desire, expressed or unexpressed. His message was a two-
edged sword because the sin and evil of oppression and injustice
coupled with the need to survive were the objects of his homiletic.
Like the prophets of the Old Testament, the slave preacher instinc-
tively knew that God and his African ancestors were friends of freedom. The preacher, often referred to as the "medicine man," was the
one person who could exhort, comfort, and tell the old, old story.
John W. Blassingame in his book *The Slave Community* devotes an
entire chapter to the culture of the slaves and, not surprisingly, discusses religion throughout. It is evident that religion and culture are
so intermingled that they are often treated as one and the same.
Blassingame says, "Clearly religion was more powerful than the master, engendering more love and fear in the slave than he could."[4]

During the early years of slavery, black folk were religious, although not necessarily Christian. This religious fervor, a combination of the sacred and the secular, inherent in what Du Bois described as "the souls of black folk," was a carryover from their African culture, whether Ibos, Dahomean, Angolans, or Shanti.[5] The slave trade and particularly the slave ship had the unintended effect of creating community out of chaos. Slaves from different tribes were suddenly thrust together in a dehumanizing situation. Out of this oppressed group arose slave preachers, who often could not read or write but were endowed with a supernatural gift of spirit and optimism. Sometimes they would imitate the master and duplicate his response, but much more often they were unimpressed by the religion their masters taught and practiced. Blassingame states:

> Most slaves, repelled by the brand of religion their masters taught, the racial inequalities in white churches, and the limitations on the bondsmen's autonomy, formulated new ideas and practices in the quarters. The true shepherd of the black flock was the slave preacher. Often one of few slaves who could read, the black preacher was usually highly intelligent, resourceful, and noted for his powerful imagination and memory.[6]

This natural, God-given talent enabled the preacher to voice the woes and sorrows of the other slaves. He spoke directly to their quest for liberation and freedom. They could "connect" to his words. His telepathic way of describing how they felt was grounded in mutual suffering and pain, and bound by the heavy chains and shackles of being perceived and treated as less than human. "Whatever the content of the sermons, the slaves preferred a black preacher."[7] They could trust the preacher and relate to the language and symbol of freedom he espoused. Although the preacher had to be careful not to anger the slave master, preaching enabled him to paint a vivid picture of heaven and hell and the prevailing oppressive social structure with a few simple strokes of the imagination. The slave hearers could read between the lines and understand that there was something liberating about the message and the messenger. The fact that this man in chains, this chattel bound by law and custom, could venture to speak what "thus says the Lord" was reason enough to hope and believe in the power of God.

Today there are black preachers who retain vestiges of the past—a past that is deeply rooted in the hearts and minds of those who dare to declare "what thus says the Lord." To a degree, the preacher is still an oratorical genius whose voice thunders like the roar of a mighty wind—one who naturally meshes style and content in a way that continues to touch the heartstrings of black church folk. When somebody says "amen," shouts, claps his or her hands or stomps his or her feet with rhythmic cadence and perfect timing, he or she is responding to the power of the Holy Spirit and the power of the voice of God, a voice heard through the black preacher. Blassingame quite correctly says,

> The black preacher had special oratorical skills and was master of the vivid phrase, folk poetry, and picturesque words. Described by many white observers as "rude eloquence" and "genuine oratory," the sermons of black preachers excited the emotions.[8]

The ability to touch the mind and heart with the eloquence of the spoken word remains a characteristic of the preacher who ministers to the masses of black folk. Church folk who are steeped in African culture want to "feel something" when the preacher preaches. They want to experience joy and sorrow, guilt and acceptance. They want to feel that God hears their cry, that in spite of their sins, they are accepted; they want to be assured that in spite of the gloom and doom of oppressive life situations, "there is a bright side somewhere." They also want the preacher's message to touch them, that is, to help them understand and fight against poverty, oppression, discrimination, and injustice. Not only that, they want the preacher to speak to their individual needs, troubles, desires, and frailties. The majority of black churchgoers today, like the slaves of the antebellum South, want the preacher to make connections between personal, individual salvation and community-wide redemption and freedom. And, after all the thinking and reflecting on the relationship between the chosen Scripture and the contextual situation, they want to "celebrate," in the language of Henry Mitchell.[9] However, it is important that we understand that celebration and cogitation must go hand in hand. They are not separate and apart from each other. Quite frankly, they are two sides of the same coin, that is, mutually related and interdependent, especially if preaching is to be liberative and transformative.

During much of slavery, especially during the nineteenth century, black preachers were forbidden by law and custom to preach the gospel, presumably because of the increase in rebellion and the insurrections of religious radicals like Gabriel Prosser, Denmark

Vessey, and Nat Turner.[10] These sanctions against the preacher can be compared to an episode concerning Jesus' disciples Peter and John, who healed the man who was lame from birth "at the gate called Beautiful." Members of the Sanhedrin court met and could not deny the fact that the man had been healed, so they punished the disciples and forbade them to speak in the name of Jesus: "and when they had called in the apostles, they beat them and charged them not to speak in the name of Jesus. . ." (Acts 5:40). The law forbidding slave preachers to preach was no more effective than the Sanhedrin's efforts to restrain Peter and John. Indeed, after Peter and John were admonished not to preach, Peter and John preached even more. Scripture says: "And every day in the temple and at home they did not cease teaching and preaching Jesus as the Christ" (Acts 5:42). Just as the Sanhedrin, the citadel of juridical power, could not constrain Peter and John, the laws silencing black preachers in the antebellum South could not be effectively enforced. Like the disciples, slave preachers felt that if they did not praise God, the rocks would cry out! And like Paul, they too could say, "Woe to me if I do not preach the gospel" (1 Cor 9:16).

Slave preachers were in a strange and unique position. They were victims of racism and double-talk on the part of the master, but recipients of love and support by the slaves. Eugene Genovese, in his book *Roll, Jordon, Roll*, says,

> The slaves preferred their own black preacher. Anthony Dawson, himself the nephew of a literate driver-preacher, said, "Mostly we had white preachers, but when we had a black preacher, that was heaven." Former slaves from Virginia recall that long after the repressive laws of the early 1830s had gone into effect the slaves demanded and got black preachers for their funerals. Charlie Meadow of South Carolina: "My favorite preacher was a big black African named Williams who came to preach in de darky church for us every now and den."[11]

Most black folk have always preferred black preachers. This sentiment is also expressed by Lawrence Levine in his book *Black Culture and Black Consciousness*. Concerning the slaves, he writes,

> No matter how respectfully and attentively they might listen to white preachers, no matter how well they might sing the

traditional hymns, it was their own preachers and their own
songs that stirred them the most.[12]

However, it is important to note that some modern bourgeois
blacks act as though they are ashamed of their heritage, in addition
to being miseducated about the present social structure with its
pandemic disinterest in the welfare of the poor and oppressed. They
are too often engrossed in television religion, the Rock Church, or
some other conservative evangelical movement overwhelmingly
dominated by fundamentalist whites. Additionally, the fact that a
growing number of blacks attend predominantly white conservative
evangelical and fundamentalist churches suggests these blacks have
a cultural identity problem, poor self-esteem, and insufficient
knowledge of the suffering and oppression of their slave foreparents.

The Priesthood of the Black Preacher:
The African Connection

In my first church, where I served as pastor for fourteen years, the
deacons were assigned a number of families to which they were
expected to minister. They were to pray, visit, and generally meet the
spiritual needs of those to whom they were assigned. This was an
adaptation of the Deacon Family Ministry Plan developed by the
Southern Baptists. However, when persons were hospitalized or
confined to their homes because of sickness, they were happy to see
the deacons, but they would always inform them that they also
wanted the pastor to visit and pray. In the black church, there is no
substitute for the pastor. The work of church officers and lay leaders
is important and necessary, but it does not replace the need for pastoral leadership. I believe that this insistence on seeing the pastor is
a carryover from the religious life and practices in the antebellum
South. Inasmuch as blacks were victims of slavery for a much longer
period than they have been free, it is reasonable to postulate that
some of the current practices in black religion are clearly African in
their origin. For example, it was not unusual for the West African
priest also to be king. Sterling Stuckey, in his book *Slave Culture,*
makes this point with clarity:

> Not surprisingly, the old Negro preacher and other religious
> leaders in the slave community were the ones who spoke for

their people whatever their ethnic origins. The authority of major religious leaders on the plantations owed much to the divine—kingship systems of West Africa and for that reason was the least likely to be questioned. Whereas the warrior-king was typical of Europe, much of Black Africa was characterized by the priest-king, which gave the religious leader a high status in slave communities. In Africa the priest was at times king, reaching his highest rung of authority, performing religious roles that determined the vital functions—presiding over harvests and mediating with ancestral spirits. The life forces were regulated by and passed through the king-priest whose importance was paramount.[13]

Religion was at the center of slave and black culture. The preacher, while often ridiculed, still retains respect and authority in both spiritual and secular matters. This is a result of his African lineage and the transmittal of certain Africanisms to life on the southern plantation. Stuckey says:

This helps explain the authority of the Black preacher through slavery and later. Except for that authority the "scattered and often clandestine" praise houses may not have surfaced without which the Negro spirituals may well not have come into being.[14]

The importance of the slave preacher is found not only in what he said, but in his willingness to say it. Because the white preacher was tailoring the gospel to sanction the policies of the state, black preachers knew that there was something blatantly wrong with a gospel that supported and justified slavery as the express or implied will of God.

The slave preacher's willingness to "stand in John's shoes" was itself an act of liberation, a testimony of God's power to bring peace to a troubled soul and a shackled body, and to ultimately "heal the land."

Preachers and Prophets: Turner, Garnett, and Jasper

These three preachers represent three different strands of liberation. Nat Turner was a revolutionary who desired to transform the system of evil represented by slavery. His actions were suicidal, and he obviously equated slavery with death. Henry Highland Garnett was an intellectual preacher who eloquently argued for black liberation, and John Jasper was more a charismatic accommodationist who preached to blacks and whites. Henry Mitchell, in his book *Black Preaching,* says, "There is no reason why the powers of a Jasper should not be combined with the Black liberation goals of Black preachers like Frederick Douglas or Henry Highland Garnett . . . or an orator like Bishop J. W. Loguen of the AMEZ (African Methodist Episcopal Zion) church."[15]

Nat Turner epitomizes the prophetic revolutionary preacher who was discontented with conditions of slavery.[16] Born October 2, 1800, the same year as John Brown, Turner is the most notorious slave preacher who ever lived on American soil. Indeed, unlike any black preacher before or since, Turner's hatred of the dehumanizing and sanctimonious institution of slavery, coupled with revelations from God, propelled him to seek freedom violently. He planned and implemented a revolt that killed nearly sixty whites before being captured and hanged in September of 1831.[17] He was a self-made preacher who was extremely intelligent and religious, and seriously bothered by the institution of slavery.

Turner's messianic prophetism impelled him to plan and to implement a strategy that could liberate and save black folk from this evil form of incarceration. While some white scholars[18] question and debate the cause and motivation of the Turner revolt, it is clear to me that he was driven by his understanding of God and the need to be free. His efforts to "set at liberty" the oppressed slaves of Southampton County, Virginia, became the most dreaded and feared prototype of the struggle for freedom. Whites across the South began to fortify their efforts to guarantee that nothing resembling the rebellion of Nat Turner would ever happen again. And they have succeeded in vilifying Nat Turner and characterizing physical violence as demonic—as if slavery were somehow nonviolent and Christian.

While Nat Turner's actions were the embodiment of liberation, there were countless others who embraced the liberation theme. Henry Mitchell points out that resistance to slavery was a distinct mark of the black preacher:

> Even under the constant supervision of Whites, and with the full awareness that there were Black informers, no Black preacher or exhorter dared preach an apparent acceptance of slavery unless he slipped in a few code reservations and encouragements to resistance.[19]

The violent revolt led by Nat Turner marked the turning point in the black struggle for liberation. Turner's visions of blood in a battle between black spirits and white spirits, in addition to other manifestations of the voice of the spirit, are symbols of his quest for liberation.[20] The visions could have been the manifestation of conflict that existed between the existential reality of oppression and injustice as evidenced by slavery and the subconscious desire to be free. Jungian psychology would suggest that the "structured unconscious" played a role in the visions of Nat Turner.[21] Moreover, Turner's acts of violence were akin to what Franz Fanon described as "a purgatory" through which oppressed people had to pass before they could achieve a fresh sense of identity.[22] As a psychoanalyst, Fanon understood the effect of oppression (colonialism) on the attitude and actions of the oppressed.

Because slaves were politically, socially, and economically powerless, Nat Turner felt that violence was the only alternative. In her essay "On Violence," Hannah Arendt says:

> Power and violence are opposites; where the one rules absolutely, the other is absent. Violence appears where power is in jeopardy, but left to its own course it ends in power's disappearance. This implies that it is not correct to think of the opposite of violence as nonviolence . . . .[23]

If Arendt is correct in saying that the opposite of violence is power, then Nat Turner's and Martin Luther King Jr.'s methods of liberation were more compatible than opposite. In 1831, blacks were perceived as chattel, inhuman, and utterly incapable of thinking and planning. So, according to the prevailing mind-set, Descartes' maxim cogito ergo sum, or any other self-affirming dictum, did not apply to slaves. Therefore, they were thought to be absolutely powerless—unable to think, read, write, plan, or act. Conversely, in 1963, Martin Luther King Jr. could negotiate, agitate, collaborate, and openly speak against the prevailing political system. The possession of this limited power, achieved over a period of almost three hundred years, was a critical variable in the success of the nonviolent method of liberation.

Nat Turner, known as the "old prophet," also felt that he was called for messianic purposes, to set at liberty the oppressed slaves (see Luke 4:18). Henry J. Young, in his book *Major Black Religious Leaders,* argues that David Walker's *Appeal* had influenced Turner in his liberation theology of action. Young explains the revolt by saying:

> Nat himself was not a violent man, but the situation of slavery, oppression, and racism forced violence upon him. He knew that violence was the only thing that would force America to take the slaves' quest for freedom and justice seriously. Not only did Nat realize this, but God realized it as well. God spoke through David Walker in 1829 and warned America that violence and bloodshed would result if the slaves were not freed.[24]

Nat Turner responded to the most vicious, violent, and hateful form of oppression and injustice to be perpetrated upon a people, American slavery. He realized that most whites had little respect for ethical arguments and moral appeals about justice for blacks. Only a radical, that is, a cataclysmic act could convince the architects of a violent social order that violence begets violence. Nat Turner's actions shocked whites and made them acknowledge that the antebellum South was not a sweet, peaceful place where black slaves were happy and satisfied with their lot, as politicians and plantation owners often portrayed the situation. Through Turner, "God was troubling the waters"[25] in tranquil, genteel, aristocratic Virginia. Young says, quite correctly, that

> the tragedy of violence that surrounded the Nat Turner revolt did not lie in the killings that Nat and his followers executed, but rather, it lay in the violence of slavery. The institution of slavery itself contained all sorts of violence.[26]

We will never fully know how many black folk were killed by the violent hand of slavery. Only in the eschaton, when "the sea [shall give up its] dead" (Rev 20:13), will we begin to know the extent of the violence suffered by our foreparents.

Like Nat Turner, Henry Highland Garnett was one of the most revolutionary preachers of the nineteenth century.[27] Born in 1815, he was influenced by the actions of Turner and the writings of David Walker. A "descendent of an African chief from the Mandingo tribe," Garnett was an educated man who escaped from slavery with his family in 1824.[28]

In 1843, Garnett addressed the Annual Negro Convention in Buffalo, New York, and made one of the most eloquent and straight-forward attacks on slavery that had ever been delivered by a black or white man. He called for violent revolution rather than moral suasion as the road to freedom and liberation. Like Nat Turner, he knew that whites had little or no respect for peaceful discussion and eloquent speeches. However, in persuading his black brothers and sisters, he argued that slavery was sinful and God did not intend for black folk to suffer. In connection with Garnett's position on slavery, Molefi Asante quotes Thomas Frazier who is quoting Garnett saying, (1) "to such degradation it is *sinful* in the extreme for you to make voluntary submission," and (2) "neither God nor Angels, or just men, command you to suffer for a single moment. Therefore, it is your solemn and imperative duty to use every means, both moral, intellectual, and physical, that promises 'success.' "[29]

Garnett could justifiably be called a liberation theologian, whose appeal included a mandate that slaves must first demand their freedom from their masters. Garnett's revolutionary rhetoric encouraged slaves to resist and never acquiesce to slavery as normative. He suggested that it was better to die than to live as slaves.[30]

While Nat Turner and Henry Highland Garnett advocated revolution by their actions and sermons, most preachers tended to be a bit more practical, bending to the reality of the social structure rather than trying to transform it violently. Nat Turner may have thought of himself as a black messiah whose duty and call was to lead black folk to freedom; however, Eugene Genovese argues that this certainly was not the norm.

> The sermons of the black preachers did not call on the people to be ready to follow a black messiah who would arise to lead them out of bondage. The deliverer of the people was to be God Himself, expressed in the image of Moses, (or Moses-Jesus) and he was to be called forth by faith. The preachers could have done no more. Their power did not rest on a charisma that made them direct political leaders; if anything, it rested on a willingness to forgo that role for a more practicable one. . . . Their great accomplishment was to bend to the actual conditions of slave life and to transform themselves into teachers and moral guides with a responsibility to keep the people together with faith in themselves.[31]

While this position is also embraced by Carter G. Woodson in his book *The History of the Negro Church,* some modern scholars, such as Gayraud Wilmore in *Black Religion and Black Radicalism,* suggest that slave preachers were agents of protest and change while simultaneously providing a unifying message to those in bondage. Samuel Proctor, whom I have studied with, talked to on the telephone, eaten with at the breakfast table, and sat beside on airlines, often says that black preachers have a long tradition of sustaining strategies for change, for freedom, for dignity, for liberation, for elevation, for true humanity—but never for willful self-destruction. Suicide was never an option.

There existed in the slave preacher a confluence of feelings, ideas, and experiences. He was both African and slave. He was free in spirit, but bound by law and custom. Nevertheless, he represented the institutional group life of those taken from the shores of Africa. W.E.B. Du Bois says:

> Some traces were retained of the former group life, and the chief remaining institution was the priest, or medicine man. He early appeared on the plantation and found his function as the healer of the sick, the interpreter of the unknown, the comforter of the sorrowing, the supernatural avenger of wrong, and *the one who rudely and picturesquely expressed the longing, disappointment, and resentment of a stolen and oppressed people.* Thus as bard, physician, judge and priest, within the narrow limits allowed by the slave system, rose the negro preacher, and under him the first Afro-American institution, the negro church.[32] [Emphasis added]

This brings us to John Jasper, described by some as the consummate preacher and self-made philosopher. Unlike Nat Turner and Henry Highland Garnett, John Jasper was mainly a black church preacher. His crude eloquence and tendency toward philosophical theology are expressed best in his sermons. Born a slave, this Richmond, Virginia, preacher was fifty years old before he achieved freedom, having preached for twenty-five years in the inhibiting and inhumane ecology of slavery.

During his slavery, Jasper's fame as a funeral preacher developed among slaves and some plantation owners throughout central Virginia. The funeral was often an all-day event because slaves could have their own preacher for them. William E. Hatcher says, "There was much staked on the fame of the officiating brother. He must be one of their own colour, and a man of reputation."[33] Jasper's reputation spread quickly because he was consumed by preaching the gospel. He was a preacher possessed by the power of the spoken word. In this connection, Virginia Adams, a woman who knew Jasper well, says, "It look like Brer Jasper couldn't stop preachin. It wuz his food and drink, an' enny time he'd git way beyond his strength."[34] Jasper was also a pastor, who led his folk to build Sixth Mount Zion Baptist Church in Richmond, Virginia. Again, Virginia Adams says, "Ah, he wuz a leader, I tell you he wuz. We never could have had our fine church if it had not bin fer him."[35]

The black masses were inspired by John Jasper's preaching and his willingness to help folk in need. He was imaginative, innovative, crudely eloquent, and apparently self-confident. Though he was unlettered and self-taught, his ability to communicate the gospel to blacks and whites was extraordinary. His most famous sermon, "The Sun Do Move," though scientifically unsound and laden with fallacies, inevitably met with mixed reviews. "To the untutored people before him Jasper was the apostle of light. They believed every syllable that fell from his lips. . . ."[36] To enlightened people who heard this sermon, "Jasper was an ignorant, old simpleton, a buffoon of the pulpit, a weakling to be laughed at. And yet hardly that. He was so . . . earnest, and . . . shrewd in stating his case, . . . that he compelled the admiration of his coldest critics."[37]

The ability to paint a picture with a simple stroke of the imagination was one of Jasper's most highly developed qualities as a homilitician. Lewis Baldwin says that "a number of writers have singled Jasper out as an extraordinary occurrence in the history of black preaching, basing their sentiments on his ability as a pictorial preacher."[38] The picture was his parable. The illustration in words was as visible to the mind and imagination as the colors placed upon the canvas by the stroke of the painter's brush. Jasper was an artist with a gift spoken not in "eloquent words of wisdom," but in the simple language of the masses who flocked to hear him.

Contextual Theology of Preaching Liberation

There is nothing that moves and inspires folk like a great sermon. It lifts persons from the low level of apathy and complacency to the heights of concern and action. The sermon preaches to my soul and I listen to hear the word of God through the voice of the preacher. The sermon frees and liberates the body and spirit of the hearer.

Most black preaching takes place in the black church, where people gather to be "fed" or to be "helped" in both a literal and spiritual way. Our preaching grows out of the situation in which we find ourselves. The context for liberation preaching is the congregation, regardless of its socioeconomic status. The middle class and the poor need to be transformed.

Traditionally, preaching in the black church has had top priority among clergy and laity. The pastor could be a relative failure educationally and morally; however, if he could "tell the story" on Sunday morning or whenever he was called upon, somehow he could always be forgiven for his failings or redeemed for his transgressions. The black church is still a forgiving and compassionate place; however, the need for spiritual and moral integrity in addition to social and political competence is a sine qua non to preaching the message of liberation and transformation. I do not believe the preacher deserves to be forgiven for failing to correlate the message of the gospel with the salvation of the community. Because the church is a much more complex institution than it was a few years ago, and society is more sophisticated even in its covert racism, the minister also has to be more adept in understanding and approaching the needs of people as he or she prepares and delivers the sermon.

Preaching is an awesome responsibility, and our modern society harbors some equally awesome realities. Understanding the magnitude and implications of this socioeconomic reality will enable the preacher to speak to the needs of folk who have their backs against the wall. Consequently, effective preaching cannot be limited to style and form or the substance of traditional theology and hermeneutics. Today, in addition to theological training, the black preacher needs to understand economics, history, and political theory in order to address the many needs of the black church. The context of black preaching is one of urban and rural poverty, joblessness, homelessness, discrimination, and to a lesser degree, black individual success, educational achievement, and economic independence. Whatever the situation, which is an overwhelmingly oppressive one for a significant percentage of black folks, I agree with J. Deotis Roberts that "theology needs to be developed in context."[39] And the context for preachers is the black church in all its diversity. The black church is both rural and urban. It is middle class and poor, often dealing with despair and hopelessness. This existential reality of the black condition is more than twentieth century existentialists like Martin Heidegger or Jean-Paul Sartre could imagine.[40] Quite frankly, the experience of many urban blacks that the church and the preacher are compelled to comprehend is more like a rendezvous with death[41] or the despair that the father of modern existentialism, Søren Kierkegaard, described as the "Sickness unto Death."

The telos for preaching liberation is to rescue many in the black community from the awesome grip of dying a slow death, sometimes self-inflicted but more often than not accompanied by the endemic pathological disinterest of the wielders of power, influence, and money. Preachers, both black and white, are compelled to prick the conscience of the oppressed and the oppressor in order that the powerful and transforming message of Jesus might be heard in ghettos, gentrified neighborhoods, suburbia, and rural hamlets throughout the nation and the world.

Prototypal Preaching and Worship for Liberation

Black preachers are master orators whose linguistic acrobatics can soar to the heights and depths of rhyme and rhythm, enabling the power and presence of God to be felt by all within the sanctuary. It is characterized by reason and theology as well as "something within"—a compelling and emotional desire to share the exciting and richly inspired word of God. Preaching and worship are tied together so intimately in the black church that there can be no authentic worship without effective preaching. Conversely, good effective preaching is enhanced by a warm, receptive, and participatory worship setting that respects and cherishes its history and culture.

Some black churches and preachers, however, are still trying desperately to imitate the style and content of traditional white Christianity. This can be seen quite vividly in the sermons and music of some who use as models the likes of Billy Graham or Robert Schuller and the music of Richard Wagner and Isaac Newton. There is nothing inherently wrong with emulating nonblack models, because we can learn from anyone. However, some seem to feel that the sermons and songs of whites are more meaningful and "religious" than the creations of black slaves or their progenitors, who have given us spirituals and gospels, songs of freedom and joy that far surpass the often bland fugues and anthems developed by our European and American masters.[42]

Black preaching is indeed exciting and jubilant, but it is also sad and reflective. It represents the ebb and flow of the Holy Spirit that correlates with the ups and downs of life. It reflects the reality of context and experience. Additionally, it is creative interplay between joy and sorrow, freedom and oppression, justice and injustice. It is art, style, form, and substance. It reflects the power of the church in the presence of the Holy Spirit. Yet, on the issue of liberation, too often, it is quite anemic and weak—diluted by the power of tradition and fear. Unfortunately, black preaching today is more evangelical than evangelistic, more soothing than troubling. It is more "spiritual and imaginative" than it is indicting of the framers of injustice and unrighteousness. Consequently, it needs to become more bold, prophetic, and searing, in both substance and form, in order to expedite the quest for freedom and social change. Preaching liberation is an ethical responsibility of both blacks and whites. To use the language of the philosopher Immanuel Kant, it is a duty! And for preachers to preach anything less is to be in complicity with sin and evil.

As a young pastor, I heard the words of one of the older gentlemen in the church that I shall never forget. He would greet me on Sunday morning or in the community barbershop during the week with the simple but powerful advice: "Reverend, preach the word!" Preaching the word means preaching liberation and freedom. It is preaching about the struggles that faced the prophets Amos, Jeremiah, and Isaiah. It is preaching about the lingering issues of injustice and oppression that faced black folk in the past and continue to face them today. It is never to forget our African roots, the slave experience in America, and, more important, the preaching of the elders.

An infinite number of pastors and teachers have preached in one way or another the essence of gospel of freedom and liberation. Black preachers in Virginia between 1880 and 1930 built many secondary schools to help African Americans get an education during the days of Jim Crow segregation. They helped to develop insurance companies and mutual aid societies in order that black people would have dignity, hope, and some economic security.

Liberation preaching is not a new phenomenon in the black church tradition. From the time of slave preachers and prophets like Henry Highland Garnett and David Walker to Vernon Johns and Benjamin Mays, the theme of freedom and liberation has undergirded the message of the gospel. There are indeed countless others who have worked in churches all of their lives trying to teach and enable their people to survive and thrive given the social and political climate of hate and indifference. While many of these preachers were not well known, their work paved the way for persons like Martin Luther King Jr., who is one of our best-known example of preaching liberation in this century.

King's sermons and lectures are the prototype for preaching liberation. He dealt with poverty, injustice, racism, and economic oppression. He also said, "The dispossessed of this nation—the poor, both white and Negro—live in a cruelly unjust society. They must organize a revolution against that injustice. . . ."[43] It would be nothing short of revolutionary for preachers, both black and white, to begin advocating liberation from the pulpits of this country. When the preacher abandons his or her ethic of comfort and complacency and begins to see the gospel as an agent of social change and transformation, the United States and the world will never be the same. Richard Lischer, in a recent article on King as preacher, says, "To black and white audiences alike, King preached a black gospel of liberation laced with the vocabulary of Personalism, popular psychology, nineteenth-century poetry, and civil religion."[44]

More than any other characteristic, King's message was liberative. The "gospel of liberation" as described by Lischer was certainly not King's gospel, but *the* gospel. King's message of social change is in absolute harmony with the spirit and message of Jesus, which demands cataclysmic change in the individual and social structure. For too long, black folk had been dehumanized and emasculated by the sword-wielding hand of injustice and indifference. They had been treated like the dirt dug from the graves of their foreparents—cast aside and spat upon. In the midst of this horrible, state-supported degradation, exacerbated by the complicity of the white church, came forth Martin Luther King Jr., preaching liberation and transformation.

Undoubtedly King's message provided the spark of hope that black folk needed to rekindle their self-respect and unify the community in the quest for freedom. His powerful preaching enabled young and old, lettered and unlettered to stand up and be proud of themselves and their slave foreparents. In the language of Paul Tillich, King gave black folk "the courage to be." Consequently, Lischer says, "King's preaching filled his black audience with courage and self-respect, and King himself modeled a new role for the black preacher and a new militancy for the black church in the south."[45]

While King's message instilled a new sense of courage and self-respect, it was not a new militant message. In many ways, it was simply a new voice telling the same old story; King's message was a variation on the theme of liberation that had been addressed earlier by preachers and leaders like David Walker, Henry McNeil Turner, Marcus Garvey, Lott Carey, Henry Highland Garnett, and, more important, by Jesus of Nazareth. Moreover, many of our parents and foreparents along with other church and community leaders were examples on the local level of what King represented nationally. When King preached, he was simply following in the footsteps of Jesus, who declared to the architects and sustainers of the prevailing social structure these immortal words of freedom:

> The spirit of the Lord is upon me,
> because he has anointed me to preach good news to the poor.
> He has sent me to proclaim release to the captives,
> And recovering of sight to the blind,
> to set at liberty those who are oppressed . . .
>
> —Luke 4:18

Preaching to the Disinherited

Preaching for the freedom of those who are enslaved by the structure and actions of society is a difficult and risky business. This is true because many in the black church, while knowing the truth of their socioeconomic and political situation, are uneasy and unjustifiably ambivalent about what they perceive as an attack on the prevailing social and economic conditions in society. Somehow there is a real or imagined fear by both clergy and laity of drawing a vocal, concrete correlation between the message of Jesus' first sermon and a pronouncement to liberate the oppressed (Luke 4:18). Certainly blacks and women, vis-à-vis other people of color throughout the world, continue to be oppressed by the many faces of indifference, abject racism, and invidious discrimination. The fact that a grossly disproportionate number of blacks are jobless, school dropouts, or working at the bottom level of employment continues to affect my understanding of the word of God or the good news and the goal of preaching.[46]

For example, I have begun to observe more vividly who does what on college campuses. I believe that probability statistics would confirm my observations that those who mow the lawns, clean the windows, mop the floors, cook the food, and type the memos and policy statements are mostly women and blacks.[47] Conversely, those who teach in seminaries and colleges, develop policy, and implement programs are mostly white. This reality is not limited to higher education but is evident in department stores, newspapers, factories, government agencies, and, yes, churches. Should not black preachers address these facts by declaring that this reality needs to change if there is going to be justice in the land? The gospel lets those who are locked out and left out know that there is a word from the Lord, and justice will prevail. Jesus often said "the first will be last, and the last will be first."

Over fifty years ago, Howard Thurman, in his most eloquent work, *Jesus and the Disinherited,* indicated that Christian religion needs to meet the needs of those who are on the periphery—those who have their backs against the wall. Thurman writes:

> I can count on the fingers of one hand the number of times that I have heard a sermon on the meaning of religion, of Christianity, to the man who stands with his back against the wall. It is urgent that my meaning be crystal clear. The masses of men live with their backs constantly against the wall. They are the poor, the disinherited, the dispossessed.[48]

Indeed, these are the people with whom Jesus identified, not the Pharisees and Sadducees or people in positions of power and authority. To whom is the preacher speaking when he develops esoteric homilies about issues that fail to address the hurt and agony of the poor masses? Has religion and the preaching ministry became so innocuous that both blacks and whites find spiritual and social comfort in attending church Sunday after Sunday without becoming committed to social change? Too often the preacher makes his flock feel content with their sins and at peace with the world, rather than forcing them to become uncomfortable and dissatisfied with the inequities and injustices that we observe, participate in, and, too often, create. Preaching liberation is a radical enterprise—a homiletic that forces critical internal assessment and external change. The effect of this kind of preaching is summed up best by Jesus himself when he says, "Do not think that I have come to bring peace on earth; I have not come to bring peace, but a sword" (Matt. 10:34). Preaching liberation is very much akin to wielding a two-edged sword. And, in the language of the preacher, I can see a flaming image that is indelibly etched in my memory describing the gospel message as "a two-edged sword, cutting sin and evil on the left and on the right!"

3

Beginning with the Word: Hermeneutics and the Centrality of Preaching

In the beginning was the Word . . .
—John 1:1

Slaves were distrustful of the white folks' interpretation of the
Scriptures and wanted to be able to search them for themselves
—Albert J. Raboteau, *Slave Religion*

The preaching of the word must itself be
the embodiment of freedom.
—James H. Cone, *God of the Oppressed*

Many activities in the two churches where I have served are brought to a close by forming a circle, joining hands, and praying. For example, at the end of a Bible study, prayer meeting, or auxiliary meeting, either by instinct or instruction, we often form a circle. Sometimes a person will ask to stand in the circle as a symbol of those who are sick or in some kind of trouble. I do not fully know why I initiate or facilitate the construction of a human circle in these church settings. However, I believe, as Sterling Stuckey suggests in his book *Slave Culture,* that this modern-day unity circle has its origin in the circles and rings that our foreparents formed on the shores of Africa and in the fields of antebellum America, where the smothering heat of the midday sun mixed with the venomous hatred of the slave master made the dog days of summer a continuous hell on earth. The circles that we form in churches today are variegated forms of the ring shout.

This shout is said to be a syncretism of African and American religious practices, manifesting itself in the forming of a circle, clapping hands, and moving one's feet and body slowly and rhythmically gradually picking up the pace. This shouting can still be seen and heard in some black churches, but for the most part, the shouting has ceased, yet the circle or the "ring" as symbol and metaphor is indelibly etched into our memory. It points to the nature and reality of our heritage and culture and to the continuation of a tradition that precedes our own embryonic formation. This religio-cultural experience has not been bound by time or space.

Black preachers have historically interpreted the gospel in the language of those who needed to hear a word from the Lord . . . in the time of trouble. The preacher, who often was quasi illiterate by traditional Eurocentric standards, could effectively communicate the word of God through the sermon. The sermon was "performed," or delivered as a unique art form utilizing imagination to cope with the reality of the black condition. The performed sermon developed by the slave preacher is the forerunner of what Du Bois describes as "Sorrow Songs" or what are generally described as spirituals or freedom songs.[1] The folk sermons of slave preachers John Jasper, Harry "Black Harry" Hoosier, and Samuel Black represent this genre.[2] Jasper's famous sermon "The Sun Do Move and the Earth Am Square" is more a prototype of the black preacher's masterful use of imagination as an interpretive tool than it is an example of sound biblical or philosophical preaching. While the facts of physics contradict the logic of the sermon's title, these facts do not limit or diminish the importance of imagination in preaching and thinking. Even its language, syntax, and grammar exemplify the poetic and artistic license often taken by the preacher. Moreover, this hyperbolic and metaphoric language is indicative of the preacher's method of describing the ways of God. Blacks who were transported from Africa brought with them the culture of their motherland. People don't lose their experience with God or the gods by being uprooted from their nation and community. Melville Herskovits, author of *The New World Negro,* was, unlike author and sociologist E. Franklyn Frazier, correct in arguing that significant Africanisms were retained by blacks who were uprooted from their motherland. Blacks adapted what they already knew and believed to their new life situation. In this sense, black people are no different from the Hebrew people of the Old Testament. For example, in the apocalyptic Book of Daniel, we can learn this lesson from the battle between Jehoiakim, King of Judah, and Nebuchadnezzar, King of Babylon. Although Nebuchadnezzar captured Daniel and the three Hebrew youngsters and transplanted them in a strange new land, changed their names, introduced them to new culinary delights, and did everything possible to assimilate them into Babylonian culture, he was not able to erase their homeland experience. They simply brought the God of their forefathers with them to Babylon! The biblical story shows that Daniel (Belteshazzar), Hananiah (Shadrach), Mishael (Meshach), and Azariah (Abednego) remained true to the God of their ancestors and the culture of their homeland (see Dan. 3:1–18). Henry Mitchell says, "'hermeneutic' is a code word for putting the gospel on a tell-it-like-is, nitty-gritty basis."[3] Black preachers have historically "told it like it was," even when they were preaching in the brush harbor [which was a place of refuge, away from the proximity of whites, where slaves could worship freely protected by the camouflage of brush and trees], slave quarters, or their own modern-day churches.

Liberation Hermeneutics

The first questions the preacher may ask are, What does this high-sounding word have to do with the liberation struggle? Why should black preachers be concerned about *hermeneutikos?* The answer lies in the fact that preachers are compelled to interpret Scripture and convey their meaning to people who sit in the pews. So, hermeneutics is a method of interpretation—a process of ascertaining meaning for a particular community at a particular time.[4] From the *Confessions* of St. Augustine to *Troubling Biblical Waters* and *Stony the Road We Trod* by Cain Hope Felder, countless theologians and social theorists have developed methodologies for understanding and interpreting God and the world.[5] However, the few who have acknowledged the importance of an inclusive and pluralistic approach to interpreting history and the Bible have been black preachers and theologians, feminist and womanist theologians, and the Latin American liberation preachers and teachers.

In liberation hermeneutics, meaning is based on one's perception of the social struggle as well as the reality of the social, political, and religious ecology. Therefore, black folks' interpretation of the Bible and their environment is not based on Hegel's historicity or Max

Weber's analysis of the social setting, but rather on an understanding of their own experience and history.[6] This experience and history have their origin in Africa, the middle passage, slavery, and the diabolical acts of injustice and discrimination that continue to be perpetrated by the architects and framers of the social structure. There is also a corollary experience that is grounded in the congregational life of black folk. This church-based experience has sustained blacks during the days of overt racism, Jim Crow laws, and other government prohibitions to authentic existence and self-determination. For example, both the Three-fifths Clause of the U.S. Constitution and the Dred Scott decision of the U.S. Supreme Court in 1857 denied and negated the ontological status of blacks.

The black preacher historically has been the theologian, philosopher, and social theorist of the church and community. Likewise, the pulpit has been the platform from which we have been taught stories about the power of God and the meaning of life. It has also been the place that has exhorted and instructed the community about how to act in order to survive the forces of oppression and injustice. Sometimes this entailed political compromise and hedging on some important issues. At other times, it was a "balancing act,"[7] but, more often than not, it was simply "telling it like it is."[8]

Hermeneutics is largely an experiential and contextual phenomenon. It involves phenomena that the subject alone may have experienced, without fully understanding the meaning and implications of the experience. It can be compared to what Paul described as "seeing through a glass darkly," because the paradigms for understanding experience are very different for those who live on the periphery than they are for persons who exist at the center of society.[9] As African American preachers, we are prone to interpret Scripture by remembering our past experiences.

It is in reviewing and studying our history that we are constantly brought face-to-face, again and again, with the cruel reality of slavery and the vile mentality of the South.[10] As blacks reflect upon these sordid, painful memories through stories passed on from one generation to another through the written and spoken word, we move closer toward a more accurate interpretation of the meaning of life for those who exist on the fringes of society—the minorities, the poor, the weak, the powerless. These are mainly the people that the preacher in the black church faces week after week as he or she attempts to make the gospel meaningful and relevant to the children of God. Certainly there are those on the periphery who do not attend church, but a significant number in church are also on the fringes of society. The fact that there is a cultural, political, and economic difference between these persons and those who inhabit the predominantly white suburban church demands that Scripture be clearly heard, taught, and preached in a way that specifically addresses this reality. The context of the sermon affects not only *what* is said; it also affects *how* what is preached is understood by the hearers.

The preacher who dares to interpret the gospel of Jesus Christ as a word to the despised and the poor has begun to expand his or her understanding of the notion of reassessment and recapitulation, not to mention justice and fairness. The black preacher who is committed to the liberation struggle must seek to hear new voices from the past—the voices of the prophets Amos, Jeremiah, and Daniel, as well as the voices of Sojourner Truth, David Walker, and John Brown. The preacher has to be able to reinterpret, revise, and redo much of what has been spoken and written in order to help people rethink their relationship to Christ and the world. He or she has to go back and delve into the pages of history to get a better understanding of the religion of our slave foreparents and their experience of God and the power of Holy Spirit. This will help him or her to understand African American religion and culture as a dynamic process of "interaction between past and present."[11] This understanding cannot be received without "circling back" to get a feel for the horror and agony, pain and suffering, joy and sorrow, despair and hope of those who journeyed on slave ships to the shores of antebellum America. This "circle of culture"[12] enables the black preacher to interpret the gospel and the current social situation in a way that speaks to the hurts and fears as well as the hopes and dreams of oppressed people in our particular community and throughout the world.

This process is a variation of what has been aptly described as the "hermeneutic circle."[13] Moreover, Justo Gonzalez and Catherine Gonzalez, in *Liberation Preaching,* say that "To be able to do liberation theology, a person must first have gone through the painful experience of this circle. . . . Liberation theology is grounded on a basic suspicion."[14] This hermeneutic of suspicion, or "ideological suspicion," as described by Juan Luis Segundo, is a prerequisite to preaching liberation. This means that the black preacher must be suspicious of much of what theology and history traditionally have said about God and the church. Additionally, it means that the Bible must be reinterpreted in view of the racism and classism that permeate Western exegesis and the practice of Christianity. For preachers, it also means that we need generally to view commentaries and other pastoral helps with renewed suspicion because the interpretations often reflect the sociopolitical ideology of the wielders of power and the proponents of injustice and unrighteousness. The use of commentaries alone, on which so many pastors depend, will not suffice if we are to preach liberation to the oppressed and oppressor. Moreover, preachers will have to read the Bible and explore theology from a more critical, open-minded, and suspicious perspective lest we too see and speak through the eyes and mouth of someone like Nebuchadnezzar's "golden image" (Dan. 3:14), or George Orwell's "Big Brother," or even America's holy writ, the Constitution, rather than through the eyes and mouth of the "God of the oppressed" or, in the language of the black church tradition, "the one who woke us up this morning and started us on our way."

The Nexus between Style and Substance

Preachers and others interested in liberation and transformation would be wise to study the Bible more closely and make an axis through Africa and American slavery before endeavoring to preach the truth to the people. This means that the preacher needs to understand the history and culture of both Africa and America as well as the impact of hundreds of years of American slavery upon our mind, body, and spirit. This odyssey through our motherland and through the slave experience is not only a necessary precondition for preaching and self-understanding, it is probably the only way that blacks will begin to understand the psychic pain and images deeply embedded in the recesses of our memories and dreams. We have been taught the ways of Western civilization, from the ancient philosophy of pre-Socratics such as Pythagoras, Heraclitus, Parmenides, Anaxagoras, and Protagoras to those of Socrates, Plato, and Aristotle. And we have learned about the fathers of the church—men such as Saint Jerome, Saint Ambrose, and Saint Augustine. While esoteric language and logical argument have occupied the minds of Euro-American preachers, blacks have generally remained mentally uninhibited and imaginative in their preaching, enabling both style and substance to come together in an ideal marriage, thus creating a union of all past and present experiences. The experience of Africa, American slavery, and twentieth-century suffering coupled with biblical stories and the teachings of Jesus create a new, vigorous, exciting, and liberating message—the sermon, preached in the black church tradition. It reflects a synthesis or a nexus of the Bible and culture, experience and hope.

Indeed, Don Wardlaw is correct when in his book *Preaching Biblically* he describes the traditional argument-oriented Eurocentric sermon as a "straitjacket for the preacher . . . and the Word of Scripture."[15] Preaching in the black church tradition has by contrast generally meshed form and content, that is, style and substance. The sermon in the black church has been an expression of freedom and artistic flair. It has been a catharsis for the preacher and people in the pew, because preaching is often a community activity, a group experience. Although some people seem to have an extraordinary ability to "think with their imagination," the preacher has raised this style of preaching to an art form that makes a statement about freedom and liberation. The existentialist philosopher Frederich Nietzsche made this point clear when he wrote that "One is artist if one experiences as *content* [that which all non-artists call] 'form.'"[16] Moreover, Wardlaw correctly asserts, "sermon form, then, becomes a hermeneutic in itself, releasing the scriptural Word among the hearers through the liberated expression of the preacher."[17] This is precisely what I am proposing. In plain and simple language, I am suggesting that style and substance are partners in preaching liberation. The way the sermon is preached—the style of delivery, the involvement of body and mind, the engagement of the audience, the rhythmic crescendos and decrescendos of the voice punctuated by staccato cadences and words uttered in musical style—all this is, to a degree, as important as the substance of what is being said. Indeed, it too constitutes a significant part of the sermon's substance. Manuel Scott of Dallas represents the embodiment of this style. Cornel West in his book *Prophetic Fragments,* says that

> Black churches permitted and promoted the kinetic orality of Afro-Americans—the fluid and protean power of the Word in speech and song along with the rich Africanisms such as antiphonality (call and response), polyrhythms, syncopation and repetition; the passionate physicality, including the bodily participation in liturgical and everyday expressions; and the combative spirituality which accents a supernatural and subversive joy, an oppositional perseverance and patience.[18]

The orality of African Americans is heard in both the sermon and in spirituals. Accordingly, E. Franklin Frazier asserts that the sermon is dramatic art that is sung much like the spirituals.[19] It is a dramatizing of the theme of liberation that we find in biblical stories concerning characters such as Shadrach, Meshach, and Abednego in the fiery furnace or Daniel in the lions' den. Not only did preaching mean dramatizing, but, Frazier points out, another qualification of the slave preacher was his ability to sing. Frazier refers to Miles Mark Fisher's work *Negro Slave Songs in the United States* when he says that "This preaching consisted of singing sacred songs . . . known as the Spirituals. The singing of these preachers and for that matter preaching among the Negro masses later has been a sort of 'moaning.'"[20] Clearly, the sermon of the black preacher embraces a hermeneutic that equates the importance and urgency of what is said to how it is said. The style of black preaching, in the mind of the masses in the church, is often as important as its substance. Therefore, the sermon represents a fusion of style and substance. It is a melding or synthesis of both elements into a message of freedom and hope that is heard not only in logical language, but also in the story retold from the Bible and experience. The sermon is shared not simply in rhetoric and speech, but it is also felt, experienced, and shared as the preacher creates what Martin Buber would describe as an "I-Thou" relationship. However, in the black church tradition, this relationship is probably better described as a "We-Thou" relationship, involving preacher, congregation, and the power of the Holy Spirit. In the black church, when style is divorced from substance, persons are quick to lose interest in the sermon and label the preacher a lecturer or intellectual. It is generally understood, albeit unfortunate, that in certain segments of the black church the word "intellectual," when used to describe the preacher or sermon, carries some negative overtones. When this word is decoded, it often means that the people in the church felt the preacher's sermon was boring or not as entertaining as some would prefer. Some will even suggest that the preacher can't preach, meaning that their understanding of preaching has been influenced by a certain style, and when this is not reflected in the particular sermonic presentation of the preacher, then he or she is often wrongly characterized. If there is a lesson learned in the years I have served as pastor and teacher of preachers, then it is probably fair to say that there is a host of persons who would not technically know the difference between a good or bad sermon. I suggest, however, that effectively communicating the gospel is a process that requires constant introspection and evaluation. On the contrary, entertainment in worship is the effort to force a response, to commercialize and bastardize that which is authentic and inherent to our culture.

Preachers who are oriented toward ideas and concepts and those who tend to be theological and philosophical in their method of putting the sermon together need to also intersperse among their messages stories that people can relate to from their own experience. The story, woven into the structure of the sermon, has the power to rescue it from boredom and abstraction, perceived or real. A good story is often the salvation of a sermon that is thought to be "above the head" of the listeners.

The story creates the possibility of rhythmic expressions. This storytelling tends to facilitate an Africanism that people relate to without knowing why they are attracted to it. The story is often a reflection on an experience with which the hearer can identify. When this happens, persons are often heard saying, "The spirit was here today!"

The performed sermon is not simply a product of the preacher's experience, study, and the quality of his voice, but it is a "call— response" activity very much akin to the practice of "lining" hymns—a tradition still found in some southern black churches where the preacher or some other person reads or sings a line of a song and the congregation follows. The sermon is really a congregational activity, a dialogue where a host of persons get involved in the preaching and hearing process. The late James Hopewell is correct in suggesting that in this sense the congregation participates in "hearing and proclaiming the gospel."[21] Also, the tuning of the sermon is quite prevalent among black preachers. When the preacher "gets into" the message, his tone and pitch change from a modulated form of monotony to a more syncopated rhythm that is in synchrony with the interspersed responses of the congregation. The spoken words "Amen and "Yes, Lord" in conjunction with "Say it, preacher" help to shape and form the message of the gospel, because the nexus of the preacher's words and the congregation's response make the sermon a communal act, that is, a product of the mind and spirit, of revelation and inspiration, of speaking and hearing. The sermon comes alive and takes shape when there is the bond of participation by both preacher and people. Again, Samuel Proctor cautions against the idea of a totally homogeneous characterization of those who constitute the church, suggesting that tradition, culture, and socialization are quite important, and race is not the major contributing factor. While this may be the case, it is important to note that one's race often determines the particularities of tradition and culture. Inasmuch as many of us have had different experiences, the black experience in America harbors its own uniqueness.

The Philosophical Approach to Preaching

Formal philosophy and hermeneutics have been dominated by the thought of white westerners who have had little or no compassion for or understanding of the condition of African Americans. Moreover, many have been quite indifferent to the existence of blacks except as slaves or servants often thought to be incapable of systematic reflection and critical analysis. This is, in effect, a denial of black existence. However, I agree with both Plato and Heidegger that the unexamined life is not worth living.[22]

Nevertheless, during years of reflection on philosophy and hermeneutics, African Americans—both enslaved and freed—*existed* as they do now. However, the eradication of American slavery went virtually unnoticed by those writing about epistemology, ontology, and ethics. I believe, like a host of unpublished black preachers, that philosophy is an integral part of social, political, and religious life. All of us think philosophically from time to time. And the black preacher is unquestionably a philosopher, because he or she has historically integrated social, political, and religious dimensions of life into the sermon on Sunday morning. But the preacher's philosophy is more pragmatic than idealistic, more practical than theoretical. The black preacher is a philosopher not in the tradition of the academy but in the tradition of our slave foreparents and of the unnamed grandmothers and grandfathers who taught us how to pray and how to live.

While the academy has to be viewed with a degree of suspicion, it certainly does not need to be abandoned. We must likewise read all sources with some degree of discrimination and suspicion. However, this does not mean that we should subjectively discount the theory that has been developed by our enemies or those who have discounted the contributions of African Americans. Not only do we come to know ourselves through the knowledge of our history, but we gain a greater knowledge of self by seeking to understand God and the world and relating that understanding to our ministry context. Accordingly, liberation hermeneutics is also a process of understanding God, the Bible, and experience and then applying that understanding to our particular lives. For the black preacher, it is the method and practice of speaking, hearing, and reading in order to decipher the liberation and transformation motifs found in Scripture, philosophy, and cultural history. Preachers then need to apply their interpretation of these motifs to their ministry. Although it is more than method or process, it is important to remember that the purpose of method, like that of preaching the gospel of Jesus Christ, is to change or transform the world. For the preacher whose goal is to free the minds and bodies of people, the message of the sermon is designed to transform both the individual and society, that is, to create a new worldview where justice, righteousness, and the liberation of the oppressed will become a reality for all of God's children. While this, like almost everything of which I am able to think, is easier said than done, I believe that there are some elements in the existentialist philosophy of Martin Heidegger that will help to interpret experience and the word more thoroughly. It can help preachers to contextualize their homiletics by focusing on the meaning of being black and out of Africa and interpreting this meaning to the church on a systematic basis. Every time the preacher preaches, he or she is involved in the hermeneutic process. The existence of blacks in a world that defines human existence in Eurocentric terms traditionally confounds both the language and process of communication. However, in communicating the gospel, the preacher is interpreting the Bible in light of his or her existence as a human being in a particular faith community. Blacks cannot accept all the details or implications of existentialist philosophy, or any Western tradition; however, some of Heidegger's and Kierkegaard's concepts are helpful as a method of interpreting human experience. The preacher's ability to extrapolate bits and pieces from their system and apply them to his or her particular experiences can be done without compromising the goal of liberation.

Heidegger's concept of *Dasein,* or human existence, which characterizes his philosophy, has applicability to blacks, whites, yellows, and others. The concept is colorless and can be applied to blacks. "Heidegger's philosophy is concerned with the question of the meaning of Being,"[23] as John Macquarrie says, "*Dasein* is never complete in its Being."

> A *Dasein* can either choose itself or lose itself; it can either exist (stand out) as the distinctive being which it is, or it can be submerged in a kind of anonymous routine manner of life, in which its possibilities are taken over and dictated to it by circumstances or social pressures. Thus there are two fundamental modes of existence: *authentic* existence, in which *Dasein* has taken possession of its own possibilities of Being, and *inauthentic* existence, in which these possibilities have been relinquished or suppressed.[24]

Preaching liberation is one means by which the preacher helps individuals and groups move from the suppression of possibility to the possession of possibility. Biblically, the possession of possibility is to say, like Paul, "I can do all things in [Christ] who strengthens me" (Phil. 4:13) or "I am sure that neither death nor life . . . will be able to separate us from the love of God in Christ Jesus" (Rom. 8:38–39). The authentic existence that partially constitutes Dasein is compatible with the concepts of faith and hope that undergird our understanding of Christology and soteriology, or Jesus' teachings and the salvation of Christian humanity.

Another of Heidegger's concepts to which I was introduced in seminary that has particular significance to the struggles of persons displaced from their homeland is *Geworfenheit,* which means "thrownness," or "the condition of finding oneself in a world, without knowing where one has come from or where one is going."[25] Blacks continue to know and, I believe, have known that they came out of Africa via the middle passage and subsequent anchorings of slave ships on the shores of Virginia, the Carolinas, and Georgia. This difficult journey placed them in a strange and hostile new world. The difficulty experienced by blacks had, thousands of years earlier, been similarly lamented by the Israelites as they sat by the streams of the Tigris and Euphrates rivers while exiled or "thrown" into Babylon. The words of the Psalmist express this feeling in poetic simplicity:

> By the waters of Babylon,
>   there we sat down and wept,
>   when we remembered Zion.
> On the willows there
>   we hung up our [harps].
> For there our captors
>   required of us songs,

and our tormentors, mirth, saying,
"Sing us one of the songs of Zion!"
How shall we sing the Lord's song
in a foreign land?
—Ps. 137:1–4a.

Like the Israelites, black slaves also sang songs of freedom and danced to sacred tunes as they gathered in a circle "symbolizing the unbroken unity of the community."[26] Sterling Stuckey also says, "The ring in which Africans danced and sang is the key to understanding the means by which they achieved oneness in America."[27] All blacks did not support or practice shouting, especially the more educated classes. African Methodist Episcopal Bishop Daniel Payne vehemently opposed the ring shout and favored an emphasis on education rather than this "heathen" form of worship. Stuckey argues that Payne's opposition was rejected by the masses because they saw this shouting as essential to their religion. In a stinging analysis of Payne's position, Stuckey states: "One can almost sympathize with Payne, despite his ignorance of African religion and its impact on the spiritual, political, and artistic life of blacks and the nation. . . . Payne's predicament in 1878 and later was that the majority of black Christians in Pennsylvania and elsewhere seemed actually to be more African in religious practice than European."[28]

This being "more African" did indeed cause Payne such concern, because he labored to rid the church of these practices. Although his efforts met staunch resistance in the nineteenth century it is fair to say that today Payne would be quite pleased that many such practices have essentially been extirpated from the black church experience. There is still shouting, but not to the extent that Stuckey describes.

While unity or oneness was not achieved during slavery nor since the emancipation, in black religion the ring shout or the metaphor of the circle enables blacks to deal with this alien land and culture. In Heidegger's phenomenology or ontological structure, "*alienation* is the condition of being diverted from the genuine possibilities of existence."[29] Slavery was the most inhumane diversion from human decency ever perpetrated upon a people. And nearly three hundred years of legal, social, and political disenfranchisement is certainly an extended diversion. The alienation of black people from their homeland has undoubtedly affected their existence. The extent of this effect will never be fully known. Quite frankly, blacks are still alienated and, as a minority, probably will always be alienated in the United States.

Søren Kierkegaard believes we come to grips with existence in the decisive encounter with the self that lies in the Either/Or dialectic of choice. For example, Kierkegaard made the choice between having an ordinary life with the woman he loved, Regina, or one of solitude and devotion to God. While he longed to live a life with Regina, he had an equally compelling devotion to God that lured him in the direction of devoutness. He argues that the choice is never so easy and reasonable as to be between good and evil, but always between rival goods, where one is bound to do some evil either way.[30] Kierkegaard's existentialism unfortunately argues that Christianity is something that concerns the individual alone and that we are all in despair, either consciously or unconsciously.[31] The only way we can cope with the reality of existence is through religion. Unlike Karl Marx, who argued that religion is the opiate of the people, I believe that black preaching is the cornerstone of black ecclesiastical religion. More important, it has been an existential prerogative that has generally reflected the choosing of life over death, even in cases like those of Nat Turner, Denmark Vessey, Gabriel Prosser, and others who went to their deaths before willingly succumbing to the awful condition of slavery. Theologian and historian Edward Wheeler suggests that their choice was indeed a choice for life because they interpreted slavery as death. Unlike Kierkegaard's existentialism, black religion has been more a community practice than an individual encounter. In the black church, salvation is both an individual and collective experience, because individual transformation demands community transformation. However, Kierkegaard's notion of "subjective truth as passionate personal commitment"[32] is a necessary ingredient in preaching liberation. The preacher has to believe and be committed to liberation in spite of what others say and do. The faith of our black fathers has never faltered because of the sin and evil of others—whether the slave masters of the eighteenth century or the architects of Jim Crowism and segregation in the twentieth century.

Preaching and the Power of the Word: From Nommo to Logos

Unlike the abstract and often esoteric elements that constitute Eurocentric philosophy, the truly Christian perspective is much more practical and concrete, grounded in the power of the spoken word. Preaching in the black tradition is a very African-oriented enterprise. Lawrence W. Levine helps to explain the African connection in his description of the slave preacher: "in addition to being a Christian preacher he was a conjurer who could 'raise the spirits' and use the charm he wore to become invisible whenever he was threatened."

> It was undoubtedly this type of preacher W.E.B. Du Bois had in mind when he wrote that the priest or medicine man was the chief surviving institution that African slaves had brought with them: "He early appeared on the plantation and found his function as the healer of the sick, the interpreter of the Unknown, the comforter of the sorrowing, the supernatural avenger of wrong, and the one who rudely but picturesquely expressed the longing, disappointment, and resentment of a stolen and oppressed people."[33]

The word, whether nommo or logos, has power; however, when coupled with language about the miracles of Jesus, its power is magnified. The fact that Jesus Christ encourages freedom for all is inherent in our understanding of his word. Preachers have to preach the gospel with prophetic passion, that is, unconditionally believing that Jesus Christ is the model for our freedom as well as the freedom of the oppressor. In the Gospel of John, Jesus . . . said to the Jews who had believed in him, "If you continue in my word, you are truly my disciples, and you will know the truth, and the truth will make you free" (John 8:31–32). Jesus Christ is the center of black preaching, and by being at the center liberation also becomes the implied goal of preaching Jesus Christ.

The black church is word-oriented, and the preacher has to be able to speak the language of the people and convey the message of the gospel not simply through the use of words or the cultural language of the people but by explicating the word of God as found in the Bible. When the people of the black church are heard saying "Preach the word," or "Stay in the word," or even "Let me hear the word today," they are encouraging the preacher to be true to the text and to have his or her sermon fully grounded in Scripture. The word is rich and powerful—revealing the presence and nature of God to the preacher (see Isa 2:1; Jer. 38:21). The word is the spoken essence of the Christian gospel (Eph 1:13; Col 1:5) and it provides hope to those who speak and hear.

Because African Americans are people who have historically communicated orally, in the black church preaching represents the most sophisticated form of communicating the gospel. While there are myriad styles of preaching that reflect the preacher's experience, education, and interests, most black preaching remains grounded in Scripture, (though not necessarily the text) which contains the liberating word of God. The prophet Jeremiah expresses the importance of the word and captures the spirit of the black preacher when he writes, "If I say, 'I will not mention him, or speak any more in his name,' there is in my heart as it were a burning fire shut up in my bones, and I am weary with holding it in, and I cannot" (Jer 20.9).

Preaching as Contextual Hermeneutics

Preaching in the church is hermeneutics in action. It is continuous interpretation and reinterpretation. Rudolf Bultmann coined the well-known term "hermeneutic circle" to describe this process. Likewise, in his book *The Liberation of Theology* Juan Luis Segundo uses the same terminology but gives it a different emphasis. He introduces the question of "ideological suspicion" in the process of interpreting Scripture. The preacher who is concerned with justice and fairness or the struggle for equality needs to also be suspicious of any theology that does not include the nature of the social and political milieu in its explanation of God and the world!

Every time the preacher stands in the pulpit, he or she is involved in hermeneutics. Preaching is hermeneutics because the sermon is an interpretation of Scripture applied to problems, issues, and experiences that face us on a daily basis. More specifically, the preacher is an experienced and practical interpreter of Scripture, because week after week he or she has to delve into the meaning of the gospel and share that meaning with others through this method of communication called preaching.

The fact that people come to church to hear a word of explanation and celebration means that the preacher is compelled to examine a range of concerns that include suffering, death, family, community, stewardship, love, justice, righteousness, evil, and so on. In other words, one should get a comprehensive understanding of the meaning of Christian faith by listening to the preacher on a regular basis.

Preaching in the African American church is a major responsibility that should not be taken lightly. This means that proper reflection, study, and meditation are needed in order to remain invigorated about the task. Moreover, I believe that the preacher should *Preach!* He should unashamedly instruct, convict, and compel persons to accept the teachings of Jesus and the liberating message of the gospel. His preaching needs to be a testimony of his own faith in and commitment to a God who is the light and salvation of life (Ps. 27:1ff.). The bold, well-informed, compassionate pastor is first and foremost an interpreter of Scripture.

Preaching as Linguistic Play

The philosopher Hans Gadamer helps us understand the act of preaching and the elements that constitute its essence by describing the nature of play. Inasmuch as the word "play" generally connotes something that is peripheral to the essence of an entity, that is, something that is more a prelude to reality than reality itself, its deeper meaning seems to elude us. Play certainly can be entertaining, as either tragedy or comedy; however, its meaning when used in relation to preaching transcends the entertainment mode and becomes more informative and transformative. Gadamer says,

> If we examine how the word "play" is used and concentrate on its so-called transferred meanings, we find talk of the play of light, the play of the waves, the play of a component in a bearing-case, the interplay of limbs, the play of forces, the play of gnats, even a play on words.[34]

It is the "play on words" that the preacher must master, with the understanding that words have power when they are based on the word of God: "In the beginning was the Word, and the Word was with God, and the Word was God" (John 1:1). Every time the preacher opens his or her mouth to preach after prayer and study, the word bursts forth with meaning that engenders faith and commitment. The act of preaching has the effect of transforming the nonbeliever into a believer and the faithless into the faithful.

Gadamer describes the nature of art when he writes,

> The implications of the definition of the nature of art emerge when one takes the sense of transformation seriously. Transformation is not change, but transformation means that something is suddenly and as a whole something else, that this other transformed thing that it has become is its true being. . . . When we find someone transformed we mean precisely this, that he has become, as it were, another person.[35]

This is akin to what Paul describes as a "new creation," and countless persons have indicated that the power of the preached word has resulted in their transformation. It is an ontological happening that results in a new personality, such that the former things have passed away; behold, all things become new. This includes society. Today, there are many who believe that our society has been transformed, especially since the days of segregation and Jim Crow.

Finally, by linguistic play we do not mean the lack of seriousness in our language usage nor do we mean a pundit-like progression of sounds without substance or words without meaning. Moreover, preaching as linguistic play does not mean that the preacher should mumble and fumble with the language, nor should he or she diminish the importance of semantic clarity. It does not reduce language to sound bites or bits of logic detached from the scriptural text and the coherence of thought necessary to the sermon's development. Linguistic play is having fun with language to the extent that this language is enlightening and transformative. Linguistic play is taking a word in its scriptural context, as Miles Jones often does, and bouncing it to and fro, cajoling it carefully and squeezing it as if it were like a lemon, savoring its elements of beauty and extrapolating from that word every possible meaning. Preaching as linguistic play is using words big and small, words that are long and short, terse and bold, known and unknown to unlock the mystery of the kingdom of God and to help those who hear the preached word become transformed.

4

Challenge and Conflict: Preaching and the Black Male

Black Preachers in America have traditionally been the oracles of retribution for the oppressor, the prophets of vindication for the oppressed, and *our most eloquent expressions of Black male power.* Rather than wait for Armageddon, preachers have led the Lord's advance guard—the downtrodden and oppressed— into the battle for freedom, justice and equality.
　　—Khephra Burns, "Preacher Power," *Essence* magazine

For I would that ye knew what great conflict I have for you, and for them at Laodicea, and for as many as have not seen my face in the flesh. . . .
　　　　　　　　—Col 2:1, KJV

The black preacher is expected to lead. However, this is not to imply that the leadership of the black preacher goes without challenge or conflict.
　　—H. Beecher Hicks Jr., *Preaching Through a Storm*

There is a universal and a particular dimension to preaching the gospel of Jesus Christ. This universality and particularity correspond to the nature of Scripture. Each scripture was written in a particular context; however, its universality is evidenced by the fact that princes and kings from the east and west, north and south have been affected by the power of the proclaimed word, which is usually based on Scripture. For example, sometimes Jesus addressed crowds by a lake; at other times, he spoke in the temple or in a boat. Likewise, Paul preached in different cities to different people with particular spiritual and social experiences. This can also be said of the prophets and other figures in the Bible.

Preaching liberation and transformation is, first and foremost, a mandate of the preacher and a responsibility of the black church. It is a necessary ingredient in self-determination and the struggle for freedom. Given the ominous condition of blacks in general and the black male in particular, it seems to me that preaching liberation can focus on the black male as a specific example of how liberation homiletics can be applied to help transform the individual and society. What can preaching do to transform this specific condition? However, before answering this question, the status of the black male needs to be determined and understood. Is he an endangered species, a victim of a grand design that will lead to extermination? Is he a mass of flesh and blood anesthetized by personal apathy and indifference on the one hand and public abuse and scrutiny on the other? These are very difficult questions that the preacher interested in liberation must try to address.

The preacher has to converse with both the oppressor and the oppressed. This dialogue should draw from the massive array of theories and ideals expounded upon by philosophers and poets, theologians, pastors, and teachers. The preacher who is concerned about the freedom of humankind and particularly the liberation of African American males uses whatever sources necessary to explicate the meaning of freedom in the propagation of the gospel. Unfortunately, there is often little practical advice to be gleaned from the works of white writers because their writing is conditioned by their own context and experience of domination. From platonic idealism to nineteenth-century existentialism, the liberation of blacks has been essentially a moot issue. Nevertheless, although people are prone to sin, ideas are prone to adaptability, so whenever I have the opportunity to interpret ideas and assertions that may be helpful to the black church and community, I do just that. I am often angered by the arrogant dismissal of everything that is nonwestern, and the callously pompous and one-dimensional hermeneutics espoused by theorists in social philosophy and theology. More often than not, this hermeneutics is impractical and detached from the experience of blacks and minorities. However, the preacher's task is to extrapolate from these ideas, theories, history, and culture some practical elements of liberation and to develop a method of freeing the oppressed through preaching the gospel.

The goal of preaching liberation, as indicated earlier, is to engender positive self-esteem in order to transform the condition of the individual and society by enabling black men and women, children and youth to hear anew the word of God and then to *do* or *act* accordingly. The mandate "Be ye doers of the word and not hearers only" is important to the preaching and practice of liberation.

The black preacher today is compelled to speak out on Sunday morning and every day of the week about the condition of society in general and the particular condition of black people—especially the black male, who is often conspicuously absent from the church and its concomitant activities. Too often we fail to address the root of the problem, which prevents us from coming face-to-face with the reality and the dilemma of the black man's condition in America. This dilemma and condition constitute the challenge and conflict of the specific ministry context for the preacher. Unlike the brothers in the street and in prison, the black preacher is both victim and healer, sharing the experience of faith and hope with those who have lost their faith and see life as a hopeless journey along the road of poverty and despair. This chapter is designed to apply liberation preaching to a particular issue that challenges the church, namely that of the black male. The bulk of the chapter is devoted to describing the condition of the black man in America as it relates to crime, education, and so on. It is my belief that we must understand the problem in a broad, multidisciplinary sense before we can address the complexity of the issues involved. Accordingly, a substantial amount of time is spent in presenting the facts as I understand them. The prescriptive focus of the chapter consists of several sermons preached with the express purpose of addressing the social pathology that grips the black male. I offer these sermons as examples of preaching liberation and transformation. This specific homiletic or type of preaching liberation is a viable method of dealing with the specific needs and concerns of the black male.

Understanding the Status and Destiny of the Black Male

The black male expressed to the nation and the world the meaning of unity and spiritual connectedness in the recent Million Man March on Washington, where Black Muslims, Christians, Jews, atheists, and others came together in peaceful harmony. As a symbol of strength and hope, this convocation of brothers and sisters was unmatched in American history. Hopefully, the march will be a prelude to change.

The condition of approximately twelve million black males in America is a complex phenomenon. It can be described by statistical data, but understood only by examining the pathos of the black community in the context of the larger society. Sociologically, the black male seems anathema. He is often portrayed by the media, police, educators, and others as dysfunctional, immature, hyperactive, a slow learner, violent, aggressive, lazy, and a host of other negatives. While the facts are alarming, the etiology of the condition is much more complex than its description.

The verdict is still out on whether systemic oppression and injustice, however subtle or covert, is the sole cause of the black male's condition. Likewise, there is no unanimity among preachers, theologians, social theorists, philosophers, physicians, educators, or policy makers regarding how the condition can be changed and the problems solved. However, most would agree that the survival of the black male means overcoming the odds—a situation that black folk have historically encountered again and again.

The black male has a greater chance of being murdered, dropping out of school, going to prison, and dying at an early age than any other group.[1] The practical implication of this is cause for alarm because without serious intervention, the demise of the black male will gradually become a reality. While some argue that there is a conspiracy to destroy black males, others suggest that the black male is destroying himself. As the debate continues, there is a prevailing torpor in the church, community, and throughout society that has allowed this issue to fester to the point of implosion. When a comparative analysis of the educational and socioeconomic status of black and white males is made, the black male seems disproportionately represented by descriptive statistics with negative connotations. I believe that the black church preaching a message of liberation that takes into account the reality of the black male's condition is one way of intervening. Certainly there are other interventions that must accompany the preaching, but preaching that focuses on the reality of oppression while simultaneously encouraging uplift, educational achievement, genuine brotherly love, and the value of respect and community unity can help to transform attitudes and actions.

Historically, society has painted a negative image of the black male. These bestowed images are the product of the dominant culture's propensity to describe the black male using negative language and symbols representative of deviant, dysfunctional behavior. The process of overcoming pandemic problems that have plagued our history, such as slavery, the Three-fifths Clause of the Constitution, Jim Crow laws, and other educational and economic barriers has given impetus to his quest to overcome the odds; however, these same past realities have had a negative affect on his progress. The way the black male has been treated historically is reason enough for him to be endangered, if not extinct.

Moreover, the condition of the black male represents a complexity of factual polarities and ambiguities exacerbated by his own uncanny ability to facilitate his destruction. To some, he is a "victim"; to others, he is a perpetrator of street crime; and to still others, he is a significant factor in the development of a permanent underclass.[2] His status is often determined by external forces that reinforce his minority status and limit the extent to which his desires for self-determination manifest themselves in pride or self-esteem. The black male is a descendant of Gabriel Prosser, Nat Turner, W.E.B. Du Bois, and Booker T. Washington. He is the son of Harriet Tubman, Sojourner Truth, and Ida B. Wells. His progenitors are people of determination whose experience is grounded in bondage and the quest for freedom. Like all men, he is both good and evil.[3] The black male is Marcus Garvey, Henry McNeil Turner, Martin Luther King Jr., Malcolm X, Samuel D. Proctor, Jesse Jackson, Benjamin Hooks, L. Douglas Wilder, and Gardner C. Taylor. But, lest I skew the facts, the black male was also a symbol of dysfunctional behavior and criminality for the Bush administration and those who practice American politics and construct public policy.

From Africa via the middle passage to the antebellum South, the black male has managed to survive. In the face of blatant legal discrimination and abject racism, supported by the sacrosanctity of the Constitution and custom, the black male continues his quest for being. But his difficulties persist. Moreover, Jewelle Taylor Gibbs and others argue that the black male is an "endangered species"[4] victimized by history, modern society, and the concomitant effects of exclusionary economics and politics. "Destruction of the Black male," argues John C. Gaston, "also means destruction of the Black family."[5] He states that "the negative aspects of popular culture and organized sports are major contributors to the destruction of the current generation of Black males."[6] Because of this, the black male is miseducated and unprepared to assimilate himself into mainstream America. More than fifty years ago, Carter G. Woodson argued that blacks had been miseducated. This miseducation continues today through, for example, the news media and even some colleges that promulgate the myth that a career in professional sports is a reasonable goal for black males. Regrettably, too many young black males believe this media hype until reality sets in, when they don't make the sports team and their educational accomplishments are too marginal to enable them to function in white-collar, skilled, and many semiskilled jobs.

Determining the condition or status of the black male is a difficult, interdisciplinary problem. It is very much a problem for theology, preaching, and the black church. A confluence of educational, political, economic, and social factors help to shape our understanding and description of the challenge and conflict that engulf the black male.

Education and the Black Male

In the United States education has often been thought to be a panacea for blacks. It has been touted as the key to success or the ticket to economic independence. Preachers historically have encouraged blacks to get an education. Although it is true that education is a necessary precondition to attaining certain levels of employment and "making it" to the top, black males have yet to capitalize upon its promises. In many ways the educational system has failed the black male in particular and the black family in general.[7]

These facts, coupled with the general educational performance record of black males, are disheartening. Black students are the lowest-achieving group in high school, and black males drop out of high school at much higher rates than other groups.[8] Additionally, William Oliver, quoting Jonathan Kozol, says that in 1985, "44% of Black males are estimated to be functional illiterates."[9] Oliver argues that social promotion perpetuates illiteracy, and refers to Robert Staples and Alvin Poussaint's research in asserting that in some large urban areas the dropout rate among black males is 60% to 70%. In 1986 this translated into 46% of working-age black men being unemployed. He further maintains that dysfunctional definitions of manhood among black males—the "tough guy" or "player of women"—manifest themselves in negative actions such as interpersonal violence and lifestyles centered on idleness, alcohol and drug abuse, and wife-beating.[10] Oliver embraces Molefi Asante's philosophy of Afrocentricity as an intervention paradigm to facilitate the transformation of the black community. The Afrocentric perspective enables black males to cherish and value the classical African worldview of unity, spirituality, and oneness with nature and humankind.[11] The lack of the perpetuation of cultural pride and public education's generally Eurocentric focus throughout the curriculum tend to negatively affect the progress of black children. David J. Dent, in his article "Readin', Writin' and Rage: How Schools Are Destroying Black Boys," says that teachers expect the worst from black males and inhibit masculinity by creating a double standard that characterizes "hell-raising" actions of white boys as typical, acceptable American behavior, but characterizes black boys who "raise hell" as deviant and delinquent—subject to discipline and punishment. Dent explains that black boys are at risk in the streets and in the classrooms of America's schools because they get the feeling that "white is always right" while they are generally suspect and thought to be wrong.[12] Dent maintains that racism and the schools' lack of instruction in African American culture and history serve to miseducate blacks.[13]

In addition to rage is a concomitant diminution of performance and achievement reflected in dropout rates and declining test scores of black males. Moreover, black males are not necessarily equipped to recognize the many faces of racism that creep into the process of education.

Indeed, the black male is being systematically destroyed by both external and internal forces. In his article "The Future of Black Men," William Strickland agrees with Jewelle Taylor Gibbs that the black male is an endangered species, suffering from a "double-edged holocaust: self-inflicted on the one hand and system-administered on the other."[14] Moreover, he contends, as do a host of other scholars, that the black male is in a crisis situation so pervasive that it is potentially deadly. He suspects that there is a conspiracy to "do away with black men as a troublesome presence in America."[15] The preacher has to counter this conspiracy with a message of encouragement and care, reiterating the value of the black male to the community and to the church.

Unquestionably, education is a critical determinant of the quality of family life. It is positively correlated with employment, income, life expectancy, social involvement, and a host of other variables. Yet education remains one of the most confounding public policy issues and practices of our time. Black males suffer disproportionately from the failures of public education. Teacher expectations and the attitudes of school officials affect performance. These attitudes and expectations are based on factors such as race, socioeconomic status, and test performance. The black church and the preacher must step in where the school fails and let the black male know that we have high expectations and it is not "cool" to fail or drop out of school.

Education Reform and the Black Male

The effectiveness of the education reform movement upon the achievement of black males is questionable. While the Great Society Programs of the Johnson administration were potentially capable of transforming the lives of blacks, they ultimately failed to do all that they set out to accomplish. The programs that focused on eradicating poverty, developing jobs, and reforming education were unable to transform these systems for myriad reasons. Both critics and proponents were confounded by the inability of government's commitment and resources to fully grasp and rectify the condition of urban America and the status of the black male. Nevertheless, the Head Start program, for example, did make an impact. It was probably the most valuable piece of the Great Society program. Benjamin Bloom, Jean Piaget, and other education theorists had already concluded that by age four a child's intelligence is half determined. This notion was contrary to the prevailing American philosophy of education, which focused on socialization during the preschool years.

The reform movement has not decreased the dropout rate, reduced low-end educational "tracking" or significantly increased the level of achievement for black males. I believe that some other intervention is necessary to assure equity and fairness in public education. The education reform movement has virtually ignored the black male, or it has pushed him further into the streets or placed him on an educational track that leads in one direction—a dead-end street with several detours along the way.

Tracking or Homogeneous Ability Grouping in Education

Black males are more likely than whites or black females to find themselves in low-level reading and math groups. "Tracking" is thought to be a systemic practice that is as much a part of the landscape of American schooling as reading and writing. It is often a subjective decision as to whether a child is a slow or fast learner and this decision is often made soon after he enters kindergarten. This decision usually leads to tracking, and the lowest track "leads right out the door." So, there is clearly a correlation between achievement, discipline, teacher expectation, the dropout rate, and the chilling practice of homogeneous grouping or tracking. There may be a causal relationship between placement in a low track and low achievement. In other words, tracking is more likely to *cause* poor performance than the reverse. Ruth Mitchell states, "From its beginnings, tracking was based on testing and on the notion that certain groups of individuals could only learn so much and go so far."[16] As an ongoing practice, it assumes that schooling is ineffective and skill levels are fixed. Mitchell bases many of her assertions on research studies performed by Jeannie Oakes and described in Mitchell's book *Keeping Track: How the Schools Structure Inequality*. Accordingly, she maintains that the current approach is based on the idea that skills precede knowledge, rather than the reverse—knowledge first, then skills.

Methods of schooling that keep black male children in one track and middle-class white children in a higher track are prima facie evidence of the inherent bias of placement testing. The myth that achievement tests are measures of cognitive ability is perpetuated by educators on every level, and black males suffer disproportionately from this pervasive educational practice. Those responsible for educating teachers will have also to be responsible for eliminating the ability-grouping ideology and practices that most educators bring to the classroom. Mitchell says forthrightly that "students placed in below-level texts virtually always score below grade level on tests." It doesn't take a course in logic or statistics to understand that regressive practices do not produce progressive results.

Blacks are disproportionately represented in low-ability groups, vocational education tracks, and educable mentally retarded classes.[17]

Black males are more likely to be in all these categories and less likely to be placed in gifted and talented programs. Most public school systems are *not* making sure that black students are learning.[18] This causes problems as these students progress up the education ladder.

From 1980 to 1984 the number of black men enrolled in college dropped by 25,300, from 393,389 to 368,089, according to the American Council on Education's Office of Minority Concerns. Fewer and fewer black men who enter college earn degrees. In 1984 black men earned 23,018 bachelor's degrees, a 10.2% drop from the 25,634 degrees earned by black males in 1976.[19] Michelle Collison quotes Reginald Wilson of the American Council on Education, who says, "We are seeing a decline in participation of Black males at every level in higher education."[20] Moreover, black males tend to drop out of college at a higher rate than black females and whites. In her book *Blacks in College* (1984), Jacqueline Fleming says that black men in predominantly white colleges were the least likely to make gains in intellectual development. Black males in college suffer from some of the same problems that confront them in high school: low expectations by teachers and failure to form informal relationships with teachers.

Finally, Jonathan Kozol's best-selling, courageous, lucid, and horrifying account of his experiences as a substitute teacher in the Boston public schools opened the eyes of the outside world to the pathological nature of racism that permeated the structure of public education. His book *Death at an Early Age: The Destruction of the Hearts and Minds of Negro Children in the Boston Public Schools* (Boston: Houghton Mifflin, 1967) chronicled the methods and practices of institutional racism in the education process. This microcosmic account reflected the pandemic inequality in public education over the decade following the 1954 *Brown* decision. Kozol, like Paulo Friere in *Pedagogy of the Oppressed* (1973), sought to teach black children by incorporating experiential knowledge into the curriculum and making efforts to truncate the dehumanizing effects of segregation in public education. However, the resistance of the policy makers and wielders of influence is more typical than Kozol's interest in effecting reform. Accordingly, Friere states, "It would be a contradiction in terms if the oppressor not only defended, but actually implemented a liberating education."[21] Both these authors argue that public education reinforces the status quo.

While some reformers argue for equality of results and transforming the educational system, other neoconservatives postulate that there is a crisis in authority, and the government is a victim of "overload." In their opinion, the responsibility of government is too great to take on the burdens of blacks and others in need of assistance. In *The Neoconservatives,* Peter Steinfels explains the meaning of this new ideology and describes those who are influencing public issues of education, crime, and welfare.

The condition of the black male is not an isolated, compartmentalized issue. Therefore, it is an issue that the preacher must confront. Moreover, the nexus between the condition of the black male and public policy issues of schooling, employment, and so on is clear-cut and straightforward. The nexus between the status of the black male and the theoretical formulations of the intellectual community is less readily discernible. I believe, nevertheless, that the message of the gospel via the preacher and the church will have to play a greater role in addressing the hurts and needs of this vital part of our community. Preaching liberation is an effort to transform individuals and society. This message needs to be developed and shared with those who have given up on black achievement and success—particularly black male achievement and success! The message of the gospel will enable these brothers to believe that individual and societal change is possible, and they can overcome the images, policies, and practices that tend to keep them oppressed.

Crime and Delinquency among Black Males

Crime has come to be defined in many quarters as black and male. Black males often grow up in "crime-ridden areas, attend overcrowded and underfinanced schools, and come from low income families."[22] These conditions may not necessarily cause criminal behavior; however they are not conducive to changing the situation regarding black male delinquency.

In the collection of essays *Young, Black and Male in America,* Richard Dembo writes in "Delinquency among Black Male Youth" (chapter 4) that a disproportionate number of black males are incarcerated in the jails and prisons throughout the United States. He states,

Importantly, although black youth constitute 15 percent of the 1984 U.S. population under age 18, they represent 45 percent, 54 percent, 68 percent, and 39 percent of the arrests for

murder/nonnegligent manslaughter, forcible rape, robbery,
and aggravated assault, respectively, among this group.[23]

While black males are arrested for committing more crimes, they
are at the same time at greater risk for being victimized by crimes of
violence. Moreover, there is a high correlation between income and
vulnerability to violent crime. Poor people are more likely to be both
victims and perpetrators of crime.

According to the Centers for Disease Control in 1985 the leading
cause of death among black males ages fifteen to twenty-four was
homicide. In 1982, the homicide rate for black males was nearly six
times greater than that for white males in the same age range. Moreover, most black males were killed by other black males whom they
knew, after an argument or in other nonfelony circumstances.[24]

It is true that a large number of black males are in jail. The majority of the inmates of maximum security facilities are black men. Statistics also show that one out of every six black males will commit a
violent crime. However, the fact that a disproportionate number of
black males inhabit prisons in Virginia, for example, and throughout the nation is directly related to social problems such as unemployment, lack of education, and a criminal justice system that often
victimizes black males.[25] Although there is a positive correlation
between these phenomena, this does not mean that there is a causal
relationship. Causality is difficult to prove outside of controlled lab-
oratory conditions.

Health and Employment of the Black Male

The health of the black male is affected by employment, and
employment is affected by health. The mental and physical health of
the black male contributes to his ability to function in his family and
society, as well as determining his life expectancy. In their article,
"Black Men, An Endangered Species: Who's Really Pulling the Trigger?" Thomas A. Parham and Roderick J. McDavis indicate that the
black male is a population at risk in the streets, in the schools, and at
home. While blacks die disproportionately from diseases, the primary causes of death among black youth is homicide, drug abuse,
suicide, and accidents.[26] Moreover, black males' ability to success-
fully negotiate the labor market is affected by the negative conse-
quences of the educational system. Because black males are more
likely to be suspended and expelled from school, placed in low-end

educational tracking, or pushed out of school altogether, they are also more likely to end up in the military or unemployed.[27]

The fact that homicide is the primary cause of death among young black males does not mean that blacks don't have serious health problems. In an article titled "Why Black Men Have the Highest Cancer Rate," the author suggests that black males die more frequently from cancer than whites because blacks are disproportionately poor and unemployed. Economic status is clearly correlated with health and employment. This article states forthrightly that

> black men have a higher rate of cancer than any other group in the U.S., and today the disease is killing twice as many black men as it did 30 years ago. Cancer accounts for about 20 percent of deaths among black men and the most common cancer that black men suffer is lung cancer. This is followed by cancers of the prostate, colon, rectum, stomach and pancreas.[28]

Lung cancer is directly associated with cigarette smoking, and "black men smoke more cigarettes than any other age-sex group. The incidence of lung cancer is 44% higher than that of white men."[29] For some reason, black males continue to smoke in spite of repeated warnings. This self-destruction or what Sigmund Freud labeled "death instinct" is another confounding variable in explicating the reasons for the prevailing condition of the black male.

Black males' lack of gainful employment contributes to the number of black families constituting the underclass. When the black man does not work, he is decimated and demoralized. Even when he does work, he is often poor, as Sar Levitan and Isaac Shapiro maintain in the book *Working, but Poor.*[30] Unemployment among young blacks has steadily increased over the past twenty years, although the general economy has consistently been said to have improved until very recently.

Unemployment among black males is directly related to urban poverty and other social dislocations. It may very well be the overriding determinant of family disruption, mental and physical health problems, and crime within and without the black community.[31]

Preaching the Liberating Truth to the People

Now, what does all this have to do with liberation preaching? Why include statistics, social and educational theories, and a long treatise on the black male? Preaching is one method of dealing with issues that confront and affect the black church, and preaching to the black male is one example of liberation preaching in today's black church. The black male is critically important to the transformation of our community and deserves special attention as an example of the need for liberation preaching. This does not diminish in any way the special problems and needs of black women in our churches and in society; however, the black male is being socially and educationally castrated, physically murdered, and spiritually maimed. The preacher must gather social data and then use the sermon as a method of addressing the potpourri of issues we face. The sermon must address what the Rev. Miles Jones calls the "situation in life or the condition of existence" and what Samuel Proctor describes as the "antithesis or the real." This means that different methodologies can be used to describe the same phenomena. In the correlation method, the condition of existence is tantamount to the antithesis of "real" in the dialectical method of sermon construction. In addressing this same phenomena in a different way, there is a constant dialogue between the Scripture text and the experiences of the black male, or between the real life condition of the black male and the ideal represented in the Scripture text. This means that there are always opportunities to address the needs of the black male through teaching and preaching, not to mention a host of other interventions. In preaching the truth, one must convey to the community the chasm that exists between the real and the ideal or the current situation and scriptural intent. Moreover, the preacher is required to bridge this gap with a sermon that is both textually sound and socially relevant. As a liberationist, the preacher is a social critic, a philosopher, and a theologian who is compelled to tackle the issues concerning the black male in our society.

The preacher must address issues of family violence, crime, and hatred by focusing on specific biblical stories. For example, the story of Joseph in Genesis (38–50) is excellent for incorporating the social statistics of the black male and utilizing our understanding of the Bible and social policy in preaching the word. I believe, for example, that a series of messages that incorporate the nuances, mood, spirit, and emotions inherent in the Joseph story will help to relate such a story to the needs and reality of the black male.

Certainly there are other methods of dealing with these issues; however, the preacher must use his homiletical skills as a method of transforming the lives of people. Indeed, the good news is not about maintaining or sustaining people as they are, but about transformation and change—sometimes incremental and at other times cataclysmic.

I have been fascinated by the Joseph story as found in the Book of Genesis. Moreover, I believe this story can be used as a means to address some of the lingering issues that engulf the minds, bodies, and souls of our black brothers. The following sermons are intended to address some of the issues that grip the black male and the entire community in the hope that within these messages the liberating word of God can be heard, and "those who hear" will no longer be the same.

The sermons "The Brotherhood Connection" and "Conspiracy and Cover-up," both preached in Second Baptist Church, Richmond, Virginia, are intended to speak to black men about the value and importance of brotherhood. These sermons allow the preacher to "zero in" on specific issues that face the black male and, it is hoped to encourage among black men a new degree of self-understanding, which is a precondition to transformation.

Liberation preaching should and does "tell it like it is." This means that the harsh reality of truth must be told as we seek to deal with the condition of black men in our communities. It is not an easy task, but it is a task that must be done if we are to reclaim our youth and rebuild our communities.

Preaching from the Joseph Story: Two Sermons

The Brotherhood Connection—Genesis 37:1–28

> Jacob settled in the land where his father had lived as an alien, the land of Canaan. This is the story of the family of Jacob.
>
> Joseph, being seventeen years old, was shepherding the flock with his brothers; he was a helper to the sons of Bilhah and Zilpah, his father's wives; and Joseph brought a bad report of them to their father. Now Israel loved Joseph more than any other of his children, because he was the son of his old age; and he had made him a long robe with sleeves. But when his brothers saw that their father loved him more than all his brothers, they hated him, and could not speak peaceably to him.

Once Joseph had a dream, and when he told it to his brothers, they hated him even more. He said to them, "Listen to this dream that I have dreamed. There we were, binding sheaves in the field. Suddenly my sheaf rose and stood upright; then your sheaves gathered around it, and bowed down to my sheaf. His brothers said to him, "Are you indeed to reign over us? Are you indeed to have dominion over us?" So they hated him even more because of his dreams and his words.

He had another dream, and told it to his brothers, saying "Look, I have had another dream: the sun, the moon, and eleven stars were bowing down to me." But when he told it to his father, his father rebuked him, and said to him, "What kind of dream is this that you have had? Shall we indeed come, I and your mother and your brothers, and bow to the ground before you? So his brothers were jealous of him, but his father kept the matter in mind.

Now his brothers went to pasture their father's flock near Shechem. And Israel said to Joseph, "Are not your brothers pasturing the flock at Shechem? Come, I will send you to them." He answered, "Here I am." So he said to him, "Go now, see if it is well with your brothers and with the flock; and bring word back to me." So he sent him from the valley of Hebron.

He came to Shechem, and a man found him wandering in the fields; the man asked him, "What are you seeking?" "I am seeking my brothers," he said; "Tell me, please, where they are pasturing the flock." The man said, "They have gone away, for I heard them say, 'Let us go to Dothan.'" So Joseph went after his brothers, and found them at Dothan. They saw him from a distance, and before he came near to them, they conspired to kill him. They said to one another, "Here comes this dreamer. Come now, let us kill him and throw him into one of the pits; then we shall say that a wild animal has devoured him, and we shall see what will become of his dreams. But when Reuben heard it, he delivered him out of their hands, saying, "Let us not take his life." Reuben said to them, "Shed no blood; throw him into this pit here in the wilderness, but lay no hand on him"—that he might rescue him out of their hand and restore him to his father. So when Joseph came to his brothers, they stripped him of his robe, the long robe with sleeves that he wore; and they took him and threw him into a pit. The pit was empty; there was no water in it.

Then they sat down to eat; and looking up they saw a caravan of Ishmaelites coming from Gilead, with their camels carrying gum, balm, and resin, on their way to carry it down to Egypt. Then Judah said to his brothers, "What profit is it if we kill our brother and conceal his blood? Come, let us sell him to the Ishmaelites, and not lay our hands on him, for he is our brother, our own flesh." And his brothers agreed. When some Midianite traders passed by, they drew Joseph up, lifting him out of the pit, and sold him to the Ishmaelites for twenty pieces of silver. And they took Joseph to Egypt.

This thirty-seventh chapter of Genesis captures much of the tension and agony that describe the family, the black male, and the relationship between brothers. The beginning of the story of Joseph, the son of Jacob, is filled with family violence and conflict. This story is an example of what we might call the dysfunctional family. Certainly this text indicates that there was the realization and feeling that the father loved Joseph more than he did the rest. Also, as the story unfolds, we encounter jealously, conspiracy, premeditation, and scheming by several brothers to kill their own brother. This story of Joseph, with all of its drama and emotion, all of the elements of a soap opera, resembles the feuds between brothers in the soap opera *Dallas,* or the rifts between certain other sensational television characters. All of the elements in this Joseph story are so real, so current, so close to our own experiences.

Today, in our own families, communities, churches, and everywhere we seem to look, we cannot escape the stress and conflict that engulf the black male. We all know the negative statistics on crime, joblessness, the school dropout rate, poor health, and a host of other problems affecting the black man in America. Inasmuch as we have been victimized by society to a large extent, there are certainly some things that we have done to ourselves. I believe that the time has come for us to "face up" to our own sin and guilt, to our own attitude and life situation, and learn how to be men of God, men with a mission and purpose, men who are responsible and committed to the cause of justice and fairness, peace and brotherhood. What is the nature of this brotherhood connection and what does it mean for us, as black Christian men, to be brothers?

First, there can be no hatred among us if we are to be a peaceful family. The story of Joseph teaches us what we should *not* do. When we learn what not to do, we are only a step away from what we should do. Joseph was a young man, probably only seventeen years old, when this story begins. The Bible tells us that Jacob loved Joseph (v. 3). He was special because he was conceived in his father's old age, and that apparently made his father quite fond of him—so much so that he made him a very luxurious robe different from the ordinary robes worn at that time. It was a unique, top-quality garment. It was what we might call "tailor-made" with the best available material. The other sons, Joseph's half-brothers, noticed how much their father cared for Joseph and they felt that Jacob loved Joseph more than he did them, so Scripture tells us that they got angry, upset, mad: "they hated him and could not speak peaceably to him" (Gen 37:4).

This sounds so much like what we see today among our black brothers. Persons live within the same family, grow up together, eat from the same table and drink from the same cup, share the same experiences, and receive the same education; yet, many of us seem to also exhibit the same behavior. *Hate* is a strong word, and it is used in most translations of this text. These brothers hated Joseph! Sibling rivalry is always a danger within families, and whenever there is more than one child, there is always the danger of being partial, of showing more love toward one than toward the others. For example, I remember growing up in a family where there were ten of us. I have four sisters and five brothers, and I would get accused of being a favorite child. While I think my father treated us basically the same, I did seek to please my parents, to make them proud and happy about my grades and work, and sometimes my brothers and sisters would get angry and upset—but never to the point of hated. At least I don't believe they hated me; but I do know how hate feels, because persons in the church have hated me and other pastors have indicated that similar feelings were expressed toward them by members of their churches. However, when we look at the world around us, at the black-on-black crime, at the violence that takes place within families; when we realize that the greatest cause of death among black men between the ages of fifteen and twenty-four is not poor health, not accidents or lack of medical care, but murder—then we really do have a lot to think about. There is a lot to think about in this city, this community, and in this church. Therefore, I am disturbed today because we have for too long sat back and let our young boys and young men go to the very gates of hell, falling into the pit of sin and evil. Yes, there is hate where it doesn't belong; yes, there is evil in our families; yes, there are misguided loyalties; yes, there are all kinds of troubles and problems. But brothers need to be brothers—connected not by hate, but by love and peace—connected not by evil, but by a mutual interest in the brotherhood of man and the quest for justice and righteousness.

Second, there can be no jealousy among us. If we are going to be men, exemplifying the attributes of brotherhood, then there is no need for jealousy. This story tells us that Joseph was a dreamer, and he told his dreams to his brothers and they hated him even more. He dreamed of binding sheaves in the field, and that all his brothers gathered around his sheaf and bowed down; and he had a second dream about the sun, the moon, and the stars bowing down before him (Gen 37:5-11). This made the brothers jealous. Jealousy, my friends, is a very destructive emotion. It keeps us from doing that which we are capable of doing because we are too busy concentrating on the accomplishments of someone else. Jealousy finds its way into families among brothers, sisters, husbands, and wives. We are often jealous of the achievements of others, jealous of material possessions, or jealous of the perceived success of others. We are by nature jealous! Sometimes we try to conceal it; we often try to hide it. Some of us even try to deny it, refute it, and do everything we can to appear that we are not jealous. However, others are like Joseph's brothers, who were openly jealous because their brother was a dreamer, a prophet with an ear toward the future. As black Christian men there is no room for jealousy among any of us. Allow me to suggest that instead of being jealous, let us be understanding; instead of being jealous, let us be compassionate; that instead of being jealous of one another, we too should become dreamers, and dream like Martin Luther King that one day we can walk together in unity and harmony, dream that we may live in a world of peace, dream that we can worship in a church where we can walk hand in hand, praying, studying, and praising God together. This day, let us dream of a church and community where men will stand up and be responsible—leading our children and supporting our women, teaching our youth the importance of moral values, educational achievement, and responsibilities. Yes, we need more dreamers like Joseph, and less jealousy like that displayed by his brothers.

Third, we need to stop killing each other as black men. In this Joseph story, we see that these brothers had gone near Shechem to pasture their flock, and Joseph went looking for them. However, when he was unable to find them, he stumbled upon a man who told him that his brothers had gone to Dothan, so he went after them. But before he could get to them, they spotted him from a distance and conspired to kill him, saying to one another, "Here comes this dreamer." Reuben, however, convinced the brothers not to kill Joseph but to cast him into a pit in the wilderness. As the story unfolds, when Joseph reached the brothers, they *snatched* him and stripped his robe from him and threw him into the pit. Then the brothers sat down to eat as if nothing had happened (Gen. 37:12–25). These brothers were a cold, terrible, calculating, conspiring bunch of hoodlums. The mere thought that they were willing to kill their own brother is bothersome and repulsive to me. But it also teaches us that we have not come much farther in our own practices of brotherhood and community. Family violence, dysfunctional families, and brother against brother in the African American community are serious issues. While I speak today, another brother "bites the dust" because of violence and drugs. We have internalized violence to the extent that it has become self-destructive. This problem is very complex, rooted in colonialism, egotism, deviant behavior, and a host of other causes. Yes, we have a problem that cannot be solved by anyone but ourselves. We are being destroyed by hatred and jealousy. Yes, we are still jealous of long robes and coats of many colors. We are harming each other indeed, killing each other over leather coats, sheepskin jackets and designer tennis shoes—consumed by jealousy and hatred.

But let me remind you today that this kind of jealousy and hatred is destructive. What we need is a new sense of understanding about God's purpose for us. As brothers and sisters, we are called to be united in love and peace, not destroyed by greed, jealousy and hatred.

Conspiracy and Cover-up—Genesis 37:29–36

> When Reuben returned to the pit and saw that Joseph was not in the pit, he tore his clothes. He returned to his brothers, and said, "The boy is gone; and I, where can I turn?" Then they took Joseph's robe, slaughtered a goat, and dipped the robe in the blood. They had the long robe with sleeves taken to their father, and they said, "This we have found; see now whether it is your son's robe or not." He recognized it, and said, "It is my son's robe! A wild animal has devoured him; Joseph is without doubt torn to pieces." Then Jacob tore his garments and put sackcloth on his loins, and mourned for his son many days. All his sons and all his daughters sought to comfort him; but he refused to be comforted, and said, "No, I shall go down to Sheol to my son, mourning." Thus his father bewailed him. Meanwhile the Midianites had sold him in Egypt to Potiphar, one of Pharoah's officials, the captain of the guard.

Last Sunday we began this series of sermons on the life of Joseph, the son of Jacob. We saw how Joseph's half-brothers, the sons of Zilpah and Bilhah (who were the wives of Jacob), were jealous of him because his father loved him. They were also envious of the "coat of many colors," or the long, luxurious robe that his father had made for him. In addition to their jealousy and envy, they also hated Joseph because he was a dreamer—a prophetic dreamer with an eye toward the future. Because of these feelings of envy, hatred, and jealousy, these brothers went so far as to plan and plot to kill Joseph; however, Reuben intervened and, instead of killing their brother, they sold him for twenty shekels of silver to a group of Ishmaelite traders who were on their way to Egypt. This brings us to the point in the story where we are today. Reuben has returned to the pit where Joseph was and realized that Joseph is gone, so this family conspiracy takes on a new more sinister dimension.

Conspiracy is an entangling network of lies, deceit, and cover-up, where one lie begets another and another, ad infinitum. We have seen it in government, from Watergate to Irangate. We've seen it in school, from the first time we began to cheat off of someone else's paper to the time we finished college. There are countless stories of athletes and others who were able to cheat in school and get their academic advisors to concur and who made it all the way through school simply for the public to find out later that they never learned the basics—how to read and write. In our families, among husbands, wives, and children, we have failed to tell the truth, piling one lie upon another—failing to believe that our children are showing signs of drug dependency, failing to believe that our teenage girls and boys are sexually active. Oh, we too are tied together in the network of self-deceit and family conspiracy. We too are caught up in a spiraling web of conflict. In many ways this is exactly what this Genesis narrative is all about. These brothers, these sons of Jacob, after selling Joseph to the Ishmaelites or Midianites, put together this scheme to convince their father that Joseph had been killed by a wild beast. So they took Joseph's robe, killed a goat, and dipped the robe in the goat's blood, and delivered the bloodstained robe to their father. This is the same robe that was the source of their initial jealousy. It is finally ruined! This sounds very much like *Murder, She Wrote*, or *Scarecrow and Mrs. King*, or a James Bond movie. This is high drama!

When the father saw the robe, he recognized it and concluded that a wild beast had indeed devoured Joseph, so he began to mourn. It is a terrible thing to deceive your own father, especially about the death of your own brother. But who can be bothered by deceit when what they had really planned was a homicide? Who cares about a

father when there is hate for a brother? A father is one who has nour-
ished and nurtured you, one who has provided for you and enabled
you to grow up without being hungry and uncared-for. Today, in
our communities, in our churches, we have witnessed sons who do
not respect their fathers, who like these boys of Jacob's, also lie and
deceive, scheme and plan in order to evade and escape the truth.

What does this initial chapter of the Joseph story tell us today?
How do we understand the relationship between Jacob and his sons?
What can we learn from this Scripture episode?

First, it is a terrible thing to sell your own brother. Although in
this story selling Joseph was the lesser of two evils, it is nevertheless
a very cold and callous thing to do. These brothers sold Joseph and
then tried to cover it up by suggesting he had been killed by a wild
animal. How wild and animalistic we, too, become when we are
ruled by hatred and jealousy. This is not hatred based on political
propaganda; it is not hatred between persons of different religions,
cultures, backgrounds, or political persuasions. This is not jealousy
based on groups' hailing from different communities; this is not
even like jealousy between the Joneses and the Browns, or the
Smiths and the Johnsons. This is not jealousy between lovers; no,
this is between brother and brother, those in the same family—the
same blood! the same father! Family problems, feuds and fights,
jealousy and hate—we find all of this in the black family today. One
son is jealous of the other, brothers are angry with the father and
upset with each other—all living in the same house or in the same
community. The dysfunctional family is a growing reality in the
black community, and we find a perfect corollary here in the Book
of Genesis. We must deal with the black-on-black crime problem
that is sweeping our nation from Virginia to the California coast.
We are plagued by black youth, men, and women who have no
respect for the sanctity of life and who have not come to understand
that the human body is the temple of God.

Yes, will we too sell our brother? Have we become so cold and calculating, so immune to the voice of God and the words of scripture
that tell us to "bear one another's burdens and so fulfill the law of
Christ" that we will sell our brothers? Every time we fail to commit
ourselves to Christian unity, I believe that we indeed sell our brother.
Every time we lie and deceive, we sell our brother. Every time we fos-
ter jealousy and hate among one another, we sell our brother. Every
time we fail to develop programs and activities for the black youth of
this church and community—procrastinating, pontificating, and

purposely doing nothing—we are selling our brothers to the world and the lure of the streets, selling them to the vices of the mind and body—enabling them to become victims of apathy and disinterest, victims of the jail cell or some other place of bondage or act of oppression. Yes, we are selling our lives, selling our brothers, selling each other for the equivalent of twenty shekels of silver.

Second and finally, this story teaches us how far some folk will go to cover up their sins. After these brothers gave Jacob, their father, the bloodstained robe and convinced him that Joseph was dead, they also comforted him in his grief. The Bible says, "All his sons and all his daughters rose up to comfort him." This is a very twisted and morally corrupt family. These sons had no scruples, no sense of responsibility, no respect for truth. They were consumed by hatred and jealousy, which was like a cancer eating and destroying the moral fiber of their conscience. If you hate someone, if you're jealous and entangled by lies and deceit—I'm here to tell you today that you need to let it go. Let it go and begin a new life in the word of God. Jesus says, "If you continue in my word, you shall know the truth and the truth shall set you free." Yes, these sons of Jacob, these brothers of Joseph, would have benefited from knowing something about Jesus, who taught about brotherly love: "Love your enemies and pray for those who persecute you."

Summary

The two preceding sermons are offered as examples of liberation and transformation preaching specifically aimed at the black male. These sermons provide the opportunity for the preacher to confront some of the issues that engulf and entangle the black male in our cities and churches. For example, in urban and some rural communities, the homicide rate for black males is alarming. Black-on-black crime, school dropout rates, and health statistics all concern us in our present context. The preacher is compelled to speak!

The condition of the black male is very complex, but we must start somewhere to address the problem and make a conscious effort to transform the negative statistics and images into positive programs that will make a difference. I believe that the challenge of preaching to the specific needs of black males is one method of intervening in this cycle of despair and destruction. It is not a cure-all, not a panacea, but an effort to turn the tide of conflict, death, and violence in order that we can hasten the day of brotherhood and peace.

5

Pressing toward the Mark:
Meaning and Method
in Textual Preaching

I press on toward the mark for the prize of
the high calling of God in Christ Jesus.
—Phil 3:14

Preaching is much more than sudorific antics, exegetical precision, or the eloquent use of one's vocal chords. Every preacher needs a method for developing textual sermons that will address issues of liberation and transformation. The dialectical method developed from the philosophical constructs of G.W.F. Hegel allows one clearly to extrapolate from a given text the essence of its meaning and apply that to our situation in life. Moreover, Samuel Proctor has perfected this method in his preachings and writings, and teaches it to his homiletics students. This method, which introduces the sermon by establishing a thesis and antithesis and then asks the relevant question needed to ultimately end by creating a synthesis. This synthesis is the result of answering a relevant question necessary to the development of the text. The more relevant the question is to the scriptural text, the clearer the sermon will be to those who hear the message.

The Triadic Movement of the Sermon

For many preachers, putting the sermon together can be either the easiest or the most complicated of acts. This results from a sermon's being either haphazardly or systematically constructed. I advocate establishing structure as a necessary precondition to sound homiletics. Quite frankly, putting the sermon together is never really easy, although some experienced preachers make it seem easy, because the result is so smooth and coherent that it empowers the hearer to change his or her life situation or to go out into the community to try to transform it.

As a practictioner of the dialectic method, I advocate its use and suggest that it is one of many methods that can address the needs of a congregation. This method can be used to develop any topic, subject, or theme. It is not confined to preaching; it can be used in any logical discourse. However, for preaching, it needs to be confined to the development of the text as reflected in the sermon subject or topic. This means that if the subject of the sermon is true to the chosen pericope, then textual integrity will not be sacrificed by the methodology or its antecedents.

Preaching, for me, was given new meaning and excitement after studying this method with one of its most prolific and eloquent practitioners. Samuel D. Proctor has explained and demonstrated the basics of the method in three of his books: *Preaching about Crisis in the Community, How Shall They Hear?* and *A Certain Sound of the Trumpet.*

This triadic movement is based on the thought of nineteenth-century philosopher G.W.F. Hegel (1770–1831). Hegel's dialectic includes thesis, antithesis, and synthesis; in his metaphysics this triad would look like the following:

Thesis: The absolute is pure being. (Ideal)
Antithesis: The absolute is nothing. (Real)
Synthesis: The absolute is becoming. (Union of real and ideal)

This means that the sermon moves from one thought to another in a fashion that can be easily followed by those who are listening. It also means that the traditional understanding of "points," especially the number of points, becomes ancillary to the development of the text. The sermon can have one major point or five points. This is determined solely by the text.

In applying this method to the sermon, after the preacher chooses a biblical text and a subject based on the text, he or she is then ready to begin the writing process. This process starts with a proposition that is an abbreviated form of what is to become the thesis. The proposition is the overall goal and task of the sermonic message. It is a projection—a prognostication. It is as Proctor says, "what you shall have said when the sermon is finished." It is also a proposal—a very brief statement of the purpose of the sermon. It is the sermon in a nutshell! In my view, this proposition should be based on the text that the preacher has chosen as the basis for the sermon, because inherent in the text is the possibility of liberation and transformation.

Textual Preaching (Dialectic Textuality)

For me, textual preaching—choosing a text and developing a subject based on the chosen text and then proceeding to develop the text in all of its fluidity and complexity—is the most essential requirement for preaching. Preaching, then, must be textual because the transformative power of the sermon is grounded in the biblical text, not in the topic or in the real-life situation, but in the ideal of Scripture. Too often the preacher will choose a text as a pretext and pretense to the real development of the scriptural text. He or she will read the text to the congregation as the basis of the sermon and too often pretend to develop the text, but will in fact develop a topic which often is out of synchrony with the chosen text. The development of a topic is quite often not indicative of preaching and does not suggest the formation of a sermon. The power of the sermon is grounded in the preacher's commitment to struggle with the text and allow the text to "speak for itself." When the preacher allows the text to speak, it will speak words of wisdom and comfort, love and compassion, freedom and hope, redemption and salvation to a faithless generation— a world in need of transformation. The sermon must be textual in all its implications, and the points or moves must flow from the text itself and not simply from general biblical literature, history, or sociology. In the following textual sermon, I seek to demonstrate the use of the dialectical method by developing a sermon that reflects liberation and transformation as the important goal of preaching.

Subject: Struggling against the Odds (A Dialectical Sermon)
Text: Mark 3:19–27

> Then he went home; and the crowd came together again, so that they could not even eat. And when his family heard it, they went out to seize him, for people were saying, "He is beside himself." And the scribes who came down from Jerusalem said,

"He is possessed by Beelzebul, and by the prince of demons he casts out the demons." And he called them to him, and said to them in parables, "How can Satan cast out Satan? If a kingdom is divided against itself, that kingdom cannot stand. And if a house is divided against itself, that house will not be able to stand. And if Satan has risen up against himself and is divided, he cannot stand, but is coming to an end. But no one can enter a strong man's house and plunder his goods, unless he first binds the strong man; then indeed he may plunder his house."

Proposition

Overcoming and defying odds is evident throughout the history of the oppressed. This fact is inherently related to the belief that good is more powerful than evil, and that Jesus is the embodiment of one who is constantly struggling against and overcoming the odds.

Antithesis

The real-life situation grounded in the meaning of the text as evidenced by the sermon subject/title, is the antithesis (the opposite of the thesis).

There are times when we find ourselves at odds with this world, with everybody around us. It's not that we set out to be different or that we make any special plans, any premeditated effort to be out of sync with our families, friends, church members, or other leaders in society. But it just happens. Sometimes you feel by yourself—all alone. I often feel out of sync with popular religious culture, and I find myself in conflict with those who have deified certain elements of tradition—often elements that have had little or no impact on our liberation and freedom. There are times when because those around us seem to be so much a part of the status quo and so comfortable with things as they are, we do feel rather alone. I imagine that this is the way Rosa Parks felt when her feet had gotten so tired and she took that seat on that bus in Montgomery. When the white bus driver asked her to move—she just said no. She was not only alone in her defiance, but she was struggling against the odds, because a black person could have been skinned alive, hung from a tree, killed in any number of ways in Alabama in 1955 for sitting while a white person was standing. I'm sure that both blacks and whites on that bus that particular day thought this woman was crazy. All the black folk who had grown up under the crushing hand of Jim Crow and the strong and stifling hand of the southern tradition of hate and evil masked and cloaked by facade of gentility and hospitality, all those black housekeepers and butlers, all the nannies and seamstresses, all the teachers and factory workers, the clerks and cooks, barbers and beauticians on that bus—both black and white—probably felt that this slender, quiet, unassuming woman was crazy, beside herself— even possessed by a demon. There are countless examples of folk who have been at odds with the prevailing powers, from Socrates to Martin Luther King Jr. Today there are those sitting here who feel alone, at odds with their families and those with whom they work, and even those in their clubs and groups and auxiliaries, all because they are trying to do the will of God, trying to live right, trying to do right, trying to bring about justice and fairness in a land "flowing with milk and honey" on one side of the street but mired in poverty on the other.

Thesis

The thesis is the ideal situation as reflected in the text, and is an expansion of the proposition.

I believe today that whenever you seek to do God's will and practice the teachings of Jesus, it will put you at odds with the world. Jesus, you see, was at odds with the world. He was always struggling against those around him whose understanding of the will of God was in conflict with his. As a matter of fact, in the Gospel of Mark, there seems to be an immediate clash of conscience and purpose between Jesus and the religious authorities. This conflict manifests itself in a struggle between the religious and social status quo and a new order. The Pharisees, scribes, Herodians—the doctors of law— are struggling to preserve the past and the present state of religious affairs, and Jesus is struggling to be himself, which is in constant conflict with the religious establishment. I don't think this is a struggle "within"—it is more a struggle "against." This is not simply an internal personal struggle like maybe Søren Kierkegaard had in choosing between love and devotion or his love for Regina and his love of God, but this is more a struggle of good against evil; it is not a struggle between two goods of equal personal interest. This is a struggle against "principalities and powers." It is a struggle against man's tendency to lie, against his proclivity not simply to deny the truth—but, as Martin Buber says, to invent something in the place of truth. This is a struggle against a lie, a struggle against spiritual treason, because "in a lie, the spirit practices treason against itself" (*Good and Evil*, 1952, p. 7). This is one invention that we all have had a hand in. Each of us has his own patent on lying, no matter how innocent or malicious. I think that the scribes, Pharisees, and other antagonists in this story tended to deny the truth, and they did it through accusation, "through questioning in their hearts," through silence, and through conspiracy. Jesus is constantly confronted by the establishment because his actions were often in conflict with their religious traditions and practices. It's a continuous struggle for him to be who he is, in the sense that the folk around him fail to understand him.

This story reminds me of our slave foreparents who, right here in Virginia, the former capital of the Confederacy, had to struggle just to stay alive; they had to struggle against the odds just to learn how to read and write. And some of us today still can't read, even with programs designed to help those with special needs such as: even with, Head Start, Chapter One, special education, and a host of other interventions. We have folk with college degrees who have not learned how to read or how to write a decent paper—not because they can't learn, but because they are often victims of systemic injustice that is often both subtle and covert. Booker T. Washington walked from West Virginia to Hampton University night and day, plagued by the constant threat of death, but he was driven, self-determined, and self-motivated. These struggles are not found just in the history of world affairs but also in the church, where tradition is often more sacred than the sacred, and the will of the people is often thought to be synonymous with the will of God. This is also an internal struggle, because the struggle against the forces of evil, against the prevailing religious and sociopolitical powers, against the establishment, against tradition, against any normative ethic or any moral value, is also a personal struggle—an internal struggle against fear and loneliness, against pain and suffering. This is a struggle of the soul, a struggle of conscience.

Black people have had to struggle against the odds in this country. From the slave ship to the battleship, from slavery to freedom, from the back of the white church to the brush harbor, from Jim Crow laws to the first civil rights bill, from the north to the south, and from the east to the west—all of us have had to struggle, from Ph.D.s to GEDs to no Ds at all. That's why I'm bothered by black neoconservatives who act like self-help is something new. Black people have always struggled to pick themselves up while law and custom keep knocking us back down. My mother and father, grandparents, uncles and aunts worked all their lives trying to help themselves and my brothers and sisters. And I have sense enough to know today that I did not get where I am on my own. I had some help from a lot of people. The poet is right: "Life for most of us ain't been no crystal stair." We have had it hard. But, in spite of the odds being against us, in spite of the struggle against evil, and envy, and injury, and ignorance, and injustice, and indifference, against all that would keep us from doing God's will, we have remained devoted, dedicated, and determined to do what's right and just and fair. Even if we have to stand alone with the odds stacked up against us, we have to be able to stand on the word of God. What does it mean for us to struggle against the odds?

Relevant Question
What does this scripture tell us about the nature and structure of this struggle against the odds?

Synthesis
The synthesis reconciles the juxtaposition that has been established between the antithesis and the thesis. This is the body of the sermon.

Well, let us lift up a few things. First, to struggle against the odds means that you cannot allow what others say about you to define who you are—that your ontological status, that your being, your "isness," that the stuff of your existence will not be determined by what folk are saying—that your understanding of yourself cannot be determined by what people are saying about you. The text says, in v. 21, "And when his family heard it, they went out to seize [or to restrain] him, for people were saying, 'He is beside himself.'" People were saying that Jesus was strange, crazy, and his relatives were no doubt believing that he was out of his mind and that he needed to be restrained. You see, we can often deal with what people say about us from a distance—with those who only know us from what they have heard. There was always a lot of gossip and hearsay about Jesus. I can imagine that people were always wondering about what made him tick, about how he could speak with authority and teach as no other teacher. People were curious and probably talked a lot about his fellowship with sinners and tax collectors, his association with those on the underside of culture, those who high society sneered at, those who were the subject of gossip and jokes, and so on, and people were also curious about his healing the lame . . . so the people were saying that he was beside himself, acting crazy. I want you to know today that when you strive with every fiber in your body and soul to do God's will, there will be those who will say that you too, are crazy, beside yourself, and they will do everything in their power to restrain you.

When even Jesus' family sought to restrain him because of what the people were saying, I am sure that caused him some anguish. But it did not stop him from doing the will of God. The will of God, however, cannot be restrained, the embodiment of his love cannot be restrained. The personification of his goodness and the grace that feeds the hungry and heals the sick cannot be restrained. Jesus cannot be restrained—you cannot hold him back, cannot check his power, cannot suppress the power of his spirit, cannot shackle, bridle, inhibit, limit, or restrict Jesus. Jesus cannot be restrained, and when his power overcomes us and we submit to his will, we too cannot be restrained from feeding the hungry or doing good—from helping and sharing the power of the good news. Sometimes, I don't want to cry, but when I think about how good God has been to me, I cannot help myself; the tears just flow. I know what the old folk meant when they sang, "I said I wasn't gonna tell nobody, but I just couldn't keep it to myself. It's like fire, shut up in my bones." Even those who are closest to us cannot be allowed to define us or to restrain us from telling the truth or helping those in need. Jesus knew that who he was was intimately tied to the will of God. What the people were saying reflected their lack of understanding; it showed how little they knew about God. The people could only describe what they thought, what they felt, what they discerned. For what they described as "beside himself" was a Jesus who was *himself*, demonstrating the attributes of God to both friend and foe.

Not only did his family believe that he was beside himself, but v. 22 says, "The scribes who came down from Jerusalem said he is possessed by Beelzebul, and by the prince of demons he casts out the demons." On the one hand, Jesus has the people or his family and friends saying that he is crazy, mad, beside himself. He is struggling against everybody's trying to define who he is, and none of them really understanding him. He's not beside himself, he is himself. We need to get beside ourselves with a vision that will lift us from comfort and complacency to a new and creative community. We need to get beside ourselves to the point where our vision for the church and community will keep us from perishing from drugs and violence, apathy and fear. We need to get beside ourselves if it will help to redeem and transform our community.

Second, struggling against the odds means that good and evil are always in conflict. They are never in complicity with each other, but are always in conflict. There is an inherent tension between good and evil. The struggle is always between good and evil. Jesus said, "How can Satan cast out Satan? If a kingdom is divided against itself, that kingdom cannot stand. And if a house is divided against itself, that house cannot stand. And if Satan has risen up against himself and is divided, he cannot stand, but is coming to an end" (vv. 23–26). Jesus teaches us a lesson in logic by showing how utterly absurd the scribes have been in saying that Jesus is possessed by Beelzebul, the prince of demons. If Jesus were possessed by Satan then he would be Satan, and Satan cannot cast himself out. *This* is absurd, *this* is what is crazy. Only the good can cast out evil. The battle with Satan is a battle against wickedness, a battle against evil, hate, injustice, unrighteousness; it is a battle of the good against the bad, love against hate, truth against the lie, justice against injustice.

This is a battle not of Satan against Satan, but of Jesus against Satan. This is a battle of the will of God against the will of the world. This is a conflict with Satan. Jesus is always in a battle against evil and sometimes even good is called evil. We are called today to fight the forces of evil with the good that God has instilled within us. We are called to fight against evil however and wherever it manifests itself. Whether it's institutional racism and injustice or personal hatred, whether it's church politics or crime—we must not be in collusion with evil.

Finally, spiritual power enables us to overcome the odds. Whenever there is a struggle in relationships, it's usually a power struggle, whether it's between individuals or principalities and powers, or husbands and wives, or nations and government, or even children and parents. And this is clearly so between good and evil, between Jesus and Satan. Spiritual power confounds the odds and ultimately overcomes the odds. Jesus says in this text, no one can enter a strong man's house and plunder his goods (utensils, tools) unless he first binds the strong man; "then indeed he may plunder his house" (v. 27). You see, no matter what his family and friends say about him, no matter what the scribes say about him, it does not affect his self-understanding, his self-consciousness, because a part of who he is is victory over Satan. There is "victory in Jesus." Satan has been mastered, but not just mastered—he has been bound, tied up! Bound, fastened, confined, constrained, restrained, cased in! Bound! You see, Jesus' spiritual power is in his righteousness, and we need to be more like him. Spiritual power is found not in flesh and blood, not in bones and fiber and muscle—not in strength, or might, not in guns or missiles, but in righteousness: "Unless your righteousness exceeds that of the scribes and Pharisees. . . . "

Only God, through Jesus Christ, has the power to bind the evil forces in this world. Satan, the devil, may be strong, but Jesus is stronger. Struggling against the odds means that sometimes you may cry in the lonely hours of the night—but you are not alone, because Jesus has already struggled against the odds and the odds have been overcome. He has struggled against evil and hate, against sin and death, against principalities and powers, and Jesus has overcome.

From Torment to Tranquillity (A Sermon Fragment)
Text: Mark 5:1–20

> They came to the other side of the sea, to the country of the Gerasenes. And when he had come out of the boat, there met him out of the tombs a man with an unclean spirit, who lived among the tombs; and no one could bind him any more, even with a chain; for he had often been bound with fetters and chains, but the chains he wrenched apart, and the fetters he broke in pieces; and no one had the strength to subdue him. Night and day among the tombs and on the mountains he was always crying out, and bruising himself with stones. And when he saw Jesus from afar, he ran and worshiped him; and crying out with a loud voice, he said, "What have you to do with me, Jesus, Son of the Most High God? I adjure you by God, do not torment me." For he had said to him, "Come out of the man, you unclean spirit!" And Jesus asked him, "What is your name?" He replied, "My name is Legion; for we are many." And he begged him eagerly not to send them out of the country. Now a great herd of swine was feeding there on the hillside; and they begged him, "Send us to the swine, let us enter them." So he gave them leave. And the unclean spirits came out, and entered the swine; and the herd, numbering about two thousand, rushed down the steep bank into the sea, and were drowned in the sea.
>
> The herdsmen fled, and told it in the city and in the country. And people came to see what it was that had happened. And they came to Jesus, and saw the demoniac sitting there, clothed and in his right mind, the man who had had the legion; and they were afraid. And those who had seen it told what had happened to the demoniac and to the swine. And they began to

beg Jesus to depart from their neighborhood. And as he was
getting into the boat, the man who had been possessed with
demons begged him that he might be with him. But he
refused, and said to him, "Go home to your friends, and tell
them how much the Lord has done for you, and how he has
had mercy on you." And he went away and began to proclaim
in the Decapolis how much Jesus had done for him; and all
men marveled. (Mark 5:1-20)

All of us who have lived long enough to reflect upon our lives have
been able to remember certain experiences of pain and anguish. We
can recollect episodes in our experiences that epitomize the presence
of pain. This anguish, this pain is a kind of torturing of the soul—a
lingering, long-lasting litany of one experience after another, of day
after day being torn and twisted apart by pain and agony. Over the
few days during the Clarence Thomas Supreme Court confirmation
hearings, this is precisely how Mr. Thomas has described this experience. He said that his confirmation process was torture, that the
dirt-mongers have smeared his name. He described what happened
to him as a high-tech lynching that was very much like being hanged
from a tree during the days of Jim Crow laws and slavery. I imagine
he felt somewhat like the man in our text who was tormented by the
evil, unclean spirit. Now, let us turn to the woman who accused him,
Anita Hill. She has no doubt been pained and anguished by the
questioning, the media, and everything that this has meant. Indeed,
they both have been tormented by the system, the process, the public scrutiny. But, in addition to their torment, we all have been hurt
and tormented. The black community, the black race, all of us male
and female—we all—every black person in America—are being tormented and tortured. This goes beyond being for or against Judge
Thomas. This public display of accusation and innuendo by two
prominent black leaders tends to harass, torture, and torment the
entire black community. But this torment is not new. We have been
tormented before, as individuals, as a community, and as a people.
From slavery to the Thomas hearings there has been torment and
torture. For some of us this torment, this pain, this anguish, this evil,
this demon has been a bruising force making us cry out for help—
for some soothing hand to heal us. And only the hand of God can
heal us, but God has many hands!

Let me tell you a story. I was riding just yesterday with my sons
Cameron and Corey in the car, and the sun was shining so beauti-

fully. As we rode along, they began to ask me about the rotation of the earth and why the sun does not destroy the earth. How could the earth be moving and yet we were not being thrown to outer space? I tried to explain it in terms of gravity and physics and the little I know of science. Then I said to Cameron, who was sitting in the front seat (they always battle about who shall sit in front and who in back)—I said, son, somehow God holds the world in balance. And Cameron said, "Dad, God has a billion hands." I thought to myself that God does have many hands—hands that can reach down and heal our bodies and comfort our souls, and hands that can soothe and caress our wounded hearts and broken spirits.

In spite of the torment that we have experienced or that we face today, whether it's racism or sexism, whether it's economic disparity or the many faces of discrimination, whether it is physical pain or mental anguish, mental cruelty, spouse abuse or family violence— whatever the torment, whether it's personal failure, sexual abuse, or harassment—if it's stealing or cheating on your husband or wife, regardless of what it is, it's still torment. Whether it is sickness or disease or some other malady that troubles your spirit and torments your body and mind, whatever unclean spirit or evil force that causes you to be like this man, Legion, whatever demon that causes you to cry out night and day, to bruise yourself, to scream for help—I want to encourage you today to realize that your torment is not eternal, not everlasting—that we can move from torment to tranquillity— that we too can be clothed and in our right mind.

"Well, tell us, brother preacher, how can we move from one pole to the other? How can I get from here to there? How can we move from torment to tranquillity? How can we move from rambling among the tombs to sitting, dressed up, clothed and in our right minds?"

Come with me now to see how this can be done. First, we have to learn the importance of worship. This Gerasene demoniac, this man with an unclean spirit, this man possessed by an evil spirit who roamed among the tombs, who could not be bound with fetters and chains because he would break them loose, this man whom "no one could subdue," this man who mutilated and caused harm to himself, recognized Jesus by seeing him from afar—and ran and *worshiped* Jesus. He bowed down before Jesus and worshiped. Worshiping Jesus was the first thing he did after seeing him. If we are going to move from torment to tranquillity we have to know who to worship.

Today, even if we are tormented by Satan himself, that is, whatever power torments us, our worship must be unto God through Jesus Christ. He recognized Jesus as the one to be worshiped. We have the same calling, the same compulsion—not to worship anyone or anything else—but Jesus—not the preacher, not the choir, not the musicians, not the building, not the history of the church, not the past, not the future. We don't need to worship any of the modern-day Baals that crop up in our churches. Our worship must be of Jesus, the lamb of God. . . . "And when he saw Jesus from afar, he ran and worshiped him" (Mark 5:6).

Second, to move from torment to tranquillity, we have to be able and willing to tell Jesus the truth. We have got to talk to him, to answer faithfully and honestly. Jesus asked the man, "What is your name? Who are you?" and he said, "My name is Legion; for we are many." He was saying, "Jesus, I feel like I'm possessed by a thousand demons.[1] [International Critical Commentary] I feel out of control." I need help from a source outside of myself!" . . .

Divine Deliverance (A Sermon Fragment)
Text: Mark 6:47–52

> When evening came, the boat was out on the sea, and he was alone on the land. When he saw that they were straining at the oars against an adverse wind, he came towards them early in the morning, walking on the sea. He intended to pass them by. But when they saw him walking on the sea, they thought it was a ghost and cried out; for they all saw him and were terrified. But immediately he spoke to them and said, "Take heart, it is I; do not be afraid." Then he got into the boat with them and the wind ceased. And they were utterly astounded, for they did not understand about the loaves, but their hearts were hardened. (NRSV)

Many of us are toiling night and day—struggling to survive in the adverse situation of an economy that has taken a downturn—struggling with family and jobs—all threatened to some extent by the politics that pervade every segment of our lives. Black people are the first to suffer whenever there is a recession or an increase in unemployment. As a matter of fact, some believe that by the time white folk declare that the economy is in recession, blacks are already in a depression. Not only do we have to struggle in society, in school, on the job, at home—even in the church there is always a struggle between good and evil, right and wrong. And these struggles are always more difficult because of fear. We fear doing right and siding with right and fairness mainly because we don't seem to understand who Jesus is for us as a people. Yes, we call his name, and we can often quote scriptures referring to him, but do we really know him well enough to emulate him—to act like him?

In this text, Jesus has sent his disciples on to Bethsaida, which was located on the shores of Lake Tiberias. Like many of us today, they were toiling and struggling to get across this very short span of the sea. They were having difficulty because the wind was against them. This wind, this force, this power was against them. This wind could have been a gale wind, or a headwind, or just a powerful force. There are all kinds of winds—some may indeed be called a "breeze," a pleasant and refreshing wind, but this was certainly not a breeze. It was an adverse wind—a contrary wind that prevented them from getting to the point or place where Jesus sent them. Oh, we have some adverse winds in the church, some contrary winds—folk who try to prevent the will of God from being fulfilled. But God controls even the wind and the waves, and, in due time, the adverse winds will cease. God will deliver us from the winds of trouble and pain. Divine deliverance is a part of the nature of God as seen in the mission of Jesus Christ. This text tells us that Jesus saw that his disciples were in trouble on the sea. He knew that they were facing a tough wind because they had been struggling all night. Their boat was being tossed and twisted by the wind and the waves and they were in trouble. They needed a deliverer. There was no need for another boat to come out there because it too would have to face the same adverse wind. There was no need really to try to summon help because it was late into the night—sometime between three and six A.M. They had been out there all night—ten to twelve hours—so they needed a deliverer, someone who would not be victimized by the wind or the waves. Well, what is the nature of this deliverance? What do these words say to us about who Jesus is and our understanding of him as Christian disciples? What does this text have to say to us as we face the winds in our lives? Well, let me lift up a few things for your spiritual consideration today.

First, Jesus comes to us in whatever way he wants. In other words, Jesus wants to save us. He doesn't want us to be in constant trouble, struggling against the wind. And, when this is the case for his children, he comes toward us to reassure us that everything will be all right. If he has to reach us by walking on water, then that is what he will do. If he has to reach us by feeding five thousand with five loaves of bread and two fish, then that's what he will do. Jesus comes to us today. Sometimes it's early in the morning, sometimes it's late at night. Sometimes it's in the heat of the day. Sometimes it's in your loneliness, sometimes it's in your hospital room, or in your family crisis—Jesus does come to us in our troubles. It doesn't matter whether we are on the sea or on land. Jesus comes to us!

Second, Jesus always has good intentions; however, we don't always understand him because we too are scared or afraid of him. The text says, "He intended to pass them by. But when they saw him walking on the sea, they thought it was a ghost and cried out; for they all saw him and were terrified" (vv. 49–50). These disciples were troubled because they saw Jesus. They were afraid, scared. Now, some of you may say that it is understandable or normal for them to be afraid because Jesus has defied the laws of physics by walking on water. Well, I think that's beside the point, because these disciples worked with Jesus, they were his right-hand men; they were his inner circle, his support team. They had witnessed his power time after time and they still did not know him. God reveals Christ to them in the midst of their struggle. Jesus meant to pass by; he wanted to pass by to reassure them—to show his divine and saving presence to them. However, instead of them being reassured, they said, "It's a ghost!" They became terrified, scared of Jesus! Are we terrified of the power and presence of Jesus? Are we afraid of the holy presence of God? Oh, we do have a misplaced fear in the church. I believe that many of us are really afraid of Jesus. Instead of being afraid of the sea and the adverse winds, we fear Jesus. Well, how do we fear the Lord, the Christ, the son of God, brother preacher? Whenever you do wrong instead of right, I believe that Jesus is a ghost in your life. Whenever we choose a lie over the truth, something is wrong; whenever you do evil instead of good, something is wrong; you fear Christ, who is the essence of goodness and love. Whenever you are terrified by love and peace in the church and in your community—something is wrong. Whenever you fail to hold Jesus Christ up as the source of our salvation and the example of what we seek to be, then Jesus has become a ghost in your life and your fears have been misplaced. Don't be afraid of Jesus—because the God I serve through Jesus Christ can show up anywhere at any time. He can show up in the choir; yes, he can show up on the deacon board; yes, he can show up on the usher board, in our homes, and in our schools. We don't need to fear Jesus—we simply need the faith to believe that he can intervene in the middle of the night or early in the morning. He can show up on the Sea of Galilee or in Galilee or in the hospital room. Yes, he can show up on Lake Tiberias or in your living room, wherever there may be conflict, hurt, pain, suffering, trouble—whenever there is a need, there Jesus is.

Third, Jesus can transform your fear into calmness. Jesus, after seeing they were afraid, said, "Take heart, it is I; do not be afraid. . . . "

Summary

The preceding sermon and sermon fragments represent the use of the dialectical method as one way of addressing issues that face the church today. Each sermon was preached in Second Baptist Church, Idlewood Avenue, Richmond, Virginia, on a Sunday morning with the purpose of providing an uplifting and transformative message to those who gathered to hear the preached word. This kind of preaching is labeled liberation preaching because it is perceived by the writer to be both uplifting and transformational, that is, providing encouragement and hope while simultaneously challenging persons to effect change in church and society.

After hearing the sermons, some church members were asked to share their opinions regarding the effects of this type of preaching on their understanding of ministry in our particular urban context. They all felt that there has been noticeable improvement as a result of liberation preaching in participation in activities that are designed to help the poor and to educate our youth and adults. For example, a food-share program has been developed during the past year and a clothing program is being developed. We have begun a tutoring program that is designed to help our youth excel in school. We are also in the process of planning to open an Afrocentric school, housed in the church, that will specifically address the needs of black children in the early childhood years. This, combined with our ministry to the homeless and our effort to enable the community to reclaim the church by opening its doors seven days a week in order to do our part in transforming ourselves and the community is the beginning of a continuous effort to make a difference.

These initiatives are the direct result of preaching and teaching about Jesus as the liberator and transformer of life and raising the level of consciousness of those in the church and community.

Notes

Preface

1. James Weldon Johnson, *God's Trombones: Seven Negro Sermons in Verse!* (New York: Viking Press, 1958), p. 14.

Introduction

1. Arthur Van Seters, *Preaching as a Social Act: Theology and Practice* (Nashville: Abingdon Press, 1988), p. 19.

2. James Cone, *Speaking The Truth: Ecumenism, Liberation, and Black Theology* (Grand Rapids: William B. Eerdmans Publishers, 1986), p. 18.

3. Ibid.

4. bell hooks and Cornel West, *Breaking Bread: Insurgent Black Intellectual Life* (Boston: South End Press, 1991), p. 136.

Chapter 1

1. Edward L. Wheeler, *Uplifting the Race: The Black Minister in the New South 1865-1902.* (Lanham, Md.: University Press of America, 1986), p. 1

2. Ibid.

3. Leonardo Boff and Clodovis Boff, *Introducing Liberation Theology* (Maryknoll, N.Y.: Orbis Books, 1987), p. 34.

4. See Gustavo Gutiérrez, *A Theology of Liberation* (Maryknoll, N.Y.: Orbis Books, 1973); James H. Cone, *God of the Oppressed* (New York: Seabury Press, 1975); James H. Cone, *Speaking the Truth: Ecumenism, Liberation and Black Theology* (Grand Rapids: Wm. B. Eerdmans, 1986); Enrique Dussell, *Philosophy of Liberation* (Maryknoll, N.Y.: Orbis Books, 1980).

5. David Buttrick, *Preaching Jesus Christ: An Exercise in Homiletic Theology* (Philadelphia: Fortress Press, 1988), p. 31.

6. Cone, *God of the Oppressed,* p. 9.

7. James H. Cone, *Speaking the Truth,* p. 24.

8. Joseph H. Johnson, *The Soul of the Black Preacher* (Philadelphia: Pilgrim Press, 1971), p. 94.

9. Ibid., p. 94.

10. See Wendell Willis, ed., *The Kingdom of God in 20th Century Interpretation* (Peabody, Mass: Hendrickson, 1987); John Bright, *The Kingdom of God* (Abingdon: Nashville, 1963); Geerhardus Vos, *The Teaching of Jesus Concerning the Kingdom of God and the Church* (N.J.: Presbyterian and Reformed, 1972).

11. Bruce Chilton and J. I. H. McDonald, *Jesus and the Ethics of the Kingdom* (Grand Rapids: Eerdmans, 1987), p. 90.

12. Justo L. and Catherine Gonzalez, *Liberation Preaching: The Pulpit and the Oppressed* (Nashville: Abingdon Press, 1980), p. 112-113.

13. Bertrand Russell, *A History of Western Philosophy* (New York: Simon and Schuster, 1945), pp. 82–83.

14. Warren H. Stewart Sr., *Interpreting God's Word in Black Preaching* (Valley Forge: Judson Press, 1984), p. 19.

15. James Weldon Johnson, *God's Trombones: Seven Negro Sermons in Verse* (New York: Viking Press, 1958), p. 46.

16. Benjamin E. Mays, *The Negro's God as Reflected in His Literature* (New York: Athenaeum, 1938), p. 80.

17. William H. Pipes, *Say Amen, Brother! Old Time Negro Preaching : A Study in American Frustration* (New York: The William Frederick Press, 1951) p. 17.

18. Zora Neale Hurston, *The Sanctified Church* (Berkeley: Turtle Island Foundation, 1983), p. 99.

19. J. B. Marsden, *Dictionary of Christian Churches and Sects from the Earliest Ages of Christianity* (London: Richard Bentley, 1854), p. 162.

20. See Karl Rahner and Herbert Vorgrimer. *Dictionary of Theology, 2d Edition* (New York: Crossroad, 1981), p. 129. Also see Mircea Eliade, editor-in-chief, *The Encyclopedia of Religion, vol. 4* (New York: Macmillan, 1987), p. 383–94.

21. Ibid., pp. 383–94.

22. See Martin Hengel, *Christ and Power* (Philadelphia: Fortress Press, 1976).

23. Cone, *God of the Oppressed*, p. 138.

24. Joseph A. Johnson, Jr., *The Soul of the Black Preacher* (Philadelphia: United Church Press, 1971), p. 86.

25. Zora Neale Hurston, *The Sanctified Church*, pp. 100-101.

26. Pipes, *Say Amen, Brother!*, p. 37.

27. Ibid., pp. 34-35.

28. Cone, *Speaking the Truth*, p. 23.

29. James Baldwin, *The Amen Corner: A Play* (New York: Dial Press, 1968), p. 10.

30. James Forbes, *The Holy Spirit and Preaching* (Nashville: Abingdon, 1989), p. 21.

31. Ibid.

Chapter 2

1. See Molefi Kete Asante, *The Afrocentric Idea* (Philadelphia: Temple University Press, 1987).

2. See Albert J. Raboteau, *Slave Religion: The Invisible Institution in the Antebellum South* (New York: Oxford University Press, 1978), and Sterling Stuckey, *Slave Culture* (New York: Oxford University Press, 1987).

3. Lewis V. Baldwin, "Black Christianity in the South in the Nineteenth Century: Its Development and Character," *Religion in the South Conference Papers* (Alabama Humanities Foundation, 1986), p. 19.

4. John W. Blassingame, *The Slave Community: Plantation Life in the Antebellum South* (New York: Oxford University Press, rev. ed. 1979), p. 147.

5. For an analysis of the culture and religion of the slaves see Sterling Stuckey, *Slave Culture,* especially chapter 1, "Slavery and the Circle of Culture," and Albert J. Raboteau, *Slave Religion.* Also, see Ulysses Jenkins, *Ancient African Religion and the African-American Church* (Jacksonville, N.C.: Flame International, 1978).

6. Blassingame, *The Slave Community*, pp. 130–31.

7. Ibid., p. 131.

8. Ibid.

9. See Henry Mitchell, *The Recovery of Preaching* (San Francisco: Harper & Row, 1977), especially chapter 4, "Preaching as Celebration," pp. 54–73.

10. See Gayraud Wilmore, *Black Religion and Black Radicalism* (Maryknoll, N.Y.: Orbis Books), 2d ed., chapter 4, "Three Generals in the Lord's Army." Also, see Wilmore, ed., *African American Religious Studies* (Durham: Duke University Press, Nilmore, ed. 1989), chapter 11, "Black Theology as Liberation Theology," by James H. Cone. For extensive studies on Nat Turner, see Herbert Aptheker, *Nat Turner's Slave Rebellion* (New York: Humanities Press, 1966),

and F. Roy Johnson, *The Nat Turner Story*, (Murfreesboro, N.C.: Johnson Publishing Co., 1970).

11. Eugene Genovese, *Roll, Jordan, Roll: The World the Slaves Made* (New York: Pantheon, 1974), pp. 261–62.

12. Lawrence W. Levine, *Black Culture and Black Consciousness: Afro-American Folk Thought from Slavery to Freedom* (New York: Oxford University Press, 1977), p. 44.

13. Sterling Stuckey, *Slave Culture: Nationalist Theory and the Foundations of Black America* (New York: Oxford University Press, 1987), p. 38.

14. Ibid., p. 38.

15. Henry H. Mitchell, *Black Preaching* (San Francisco: Harper & Row, 1979), p. 135.

16. Turner is generally described as a prophet by Stephen B. Oates in *The Fires of Jubilee: Nat Turner's Fierce Rebellion* (New York: Harper & Row, 1975), F. Roy Johnson in *The Nat Turner Story*, and Eugene Genovese in *Roll, Jordon, Roll*.

17. Some sources say that Turner and his party killed fifty-five whites, others say sixty. See F. Roy Johnson, *The Nat Turner Story*, and Aptheker, *Nat Turner's Slave Rebellion*.

18. See Aptheker, *Nat Turner's Rebellion*, pp. 38ff.

19. Henry H. Mitchell, *Black Belief: Folk Beliefs of Blacks in America and West Africa* (New York: Harper & Row, 1975), p. 33.

20. Aptheker, *Nat Turner's Rebellion*, p. 136.

21. See C. G. Jung, *Psychological Types* (Princeton, N.J.: Princeton University Press, 1971).

22. See Franz Fanon, "Violence and Liberation," in James A. Ogilvy, ed. *Self and World: Readings in Philosophy* (New York: Harcourt, Brace, Jovanovich, 1981), pp. 339–45.

23. Hannah Arendt, "On Violence," p. 355.

24. Henry J. Young, *Major Black Religious Leaders* (Nashville: Abingdon Press, 1977), p. 56.

25. See Cain Hope Felder, *Troubling Biblical Waters: Race, Class and Family* (Maryknoll, N.Y.: Orbis Books, 1989).

26. Young, *Major Black Religious Leaders*, p. 58.

27. Eugene Genovese argues that there were few "prophets" during slavery and the historical record attests to the accuracy of his assertion. However, the slave preacher, more than anyone else, ran the risk of being killed for teaching and preaching a gospel that was contrary to the slave master's will. Genovese states, in *Roll, Jordon, Roll*, "The preachers preached; they did not prophesy, except in the

narrowest meaning of the word. The somber political implications of black folk religion—to recall Fanon's hostility—and the long shadow they have cast over the black liberation movement were reflected in the rarity of prophets and the virtual absence of a prophetic tradition among the slaves. To be sure, the generalization is shorthand. Nat Turner was rightly called 'Ole Prophet Nat' and other such revolutionary prophets appeared from time to time" (p. 272).

28. Young, *Major Black Religious Leaders,* pp. 85–86.

29. Asante, *The Afrocentric Idea,* p. 144.

30. Young, *Major Black Religious Leaders,* p. 98.

31. Genovese, *Roll, Jordon, Roll,* pp. 272–73.

32. W.E.B. Du Bois, *The Souls of Black Folk in Three Negro Classics,* p. 442.

33. William Hatcher, *John Jasper: The Unmatched Negro Philosopher and Preacher* (Fleming H. Revell, 1908), p. 37.

34. Ibid., p. 81.

35. Ibid., pp. 86–87.

36. Ibid., p. 128.

37. Ibid.

38. Lewis V. Baldwin, "Git Right Wit Gawd! The Slave Preacher and the Folk Sermon as Revealed through the Channels of Afro-American Folk Sources." Unpublished paper.

39. J. Deotis Roberts, *Black Theology in Dialogue* (Philadelphia: Westminster Press, 1987), p. 15.

40. For general introductory information about Heidegger, Sartre, and other existentialists, see Robert C. Solomon, *The Big Questions: A Short Introduction to Philosophy,* 3d ed. (New York: Harcourt, Brace, Jovanovich, 1990).

41. See the poem "I Have a Rendezvous with Death," by Alan Seeger, in *Prose and Poetry of America,* H. Ward McGraw, ed. (Syracuse: L. W. Singer, 1935), p. 470.

42. See Mark P. Bangert, "Black Gospel and Spirituals: A Primer," *Currents in Theology and Missions* (June 1989), vol. 16, no. 3, pp. 173–79.

43. Martin Luther King Jr., *The Trumpet of Conscience* (San Francisco: Harper & Row, 1968), p. 59.

44. Richard Lischer, "The Word that Moves," *Theology Today,* vol. XLVI, no. 2 (July 1989), p. 179.

45. Ibid., p. 180.

46. See Sar Levitan and Isaac Shapiro, *Working, but Poor* (Balti-

more: Johns Hopkins University Press, 1987), and William Dunn, "Picture for Blacks: "Still Bleak," *USA Today*, July 28–30, 1989, p. 1A. Dunn's article points out that "blacks constitute 12.3% of the U.S. population; however, 33% live in poverty up from a low of 30% in 1974. The USA's overall poverty rate is 13.5%. Median 1987 income of black families was $18,098—56% of whites' $32,274. Black unemployment was 11.7% in 1988 vs. an overall 5.5%." For more information on this topic, see Michael Harrington, *The Other America: Poverty in the United States* (New York: Macmillan, 1962), and *The Twilight of Capitalism* (New York: Simon and Schuster, 1976).

47. See Levitan and Shapiro, *Working, but Poor*.

48. Howard Thurman, *Jesus and the Disinherited* (Richmond, Ind.: Friends United Press, 1981), p. 13.

Chapter 3

1. For an in-depth analysis of the performed, chanted, and sung folk sermon, see Gerald L. Davis, *I got the Word in me and I can sing it, you know: A Study of the Performed African-American Sermon* (Philadelphia: University of Pennsylvania Press, 1985). See also Lewis V. Baldwin, " 'Git Right Wit Gaud': The Slave Preacher and the Folk Sermon as Revealed through the Channels of Afro-American Folk Sources" (Evanston, Ill.: Northwestern University Department of History, unpublished research paper).

2. Ibid. Baldwin says, "Every slave preacher knew the power of a strong element of chanting in his preaching and many became men of great status because they mastered the art of 'singing the gospel.'"

3. Henry H. Mitchell, *Black Preaching* (San Francisco: Harper & Row, 1979), p. 30.

4. See Zygmunt Bauman, *Hermeneutics and Social Science* (New York: Columbia University Press, 1978).

5. Through the centuries hermeneutics has developed from being a branch of philology to becoming a distinct yet broad-based analytical process encompassing various approaches, from historiography to the sociology of knowledge.

6. While social, philosophical, and political theorists including Karl Marx, Max Weber, Auguste Comte, Ludwig Wittgenstein, Robert Nozick, John Rawls, and others are helpful in analyzing the social structure, they must never be too heavily depended upon, because their perspectives are also Eurocentric and not necessarily conducive to black liberation. While I am open to the views of any analyst, theorist, or practitioner in the struggle for liberation, I real-

ize the need for caution and suspicion as we seek to incorporate the views of others in this unique struggle. Also see Molefi Kete Asante, *The Afrocentric Idea* (Philadelphia: Temple University Press, 1987). One of the most profound statements warning blacks against the overuse and uncritical acceptance of Marxism as helpful in developing Afrocentric concepts and methods is made by Asante, because, he says, "it, too, is a product of a Eurocentric consciousness that excludes the historical and cultural perspectives of Africa. . . . because it emerged from the Western consciousness. Marxism is mechanistic in its approach to social understanding and development, and it has often adopted forms of social Darwinism when explaining cultural and social phenomena. What makes Afrocentric concepts more inclusive is that they seek to reorient our world view in ways that challenge social Darwinism, capitalism, and most forms of Marxist theory—all of which are grounded in their own particularity."

7. See Carter G. Woodson, *The History of the Negro Church* (Washington, D.C.: Associated Publishers, 1945).

8. See Mitchell, *Black Preaching.*

9. See Enrique Dussel, *Philosophy of Liberation* (New York: Orbis Books, 1980).

10. See W. J. Cash, *The Mind of the South* (New York: Alfred A. Knopf, 1962).

11. Lawrence W. Levine, *Black Culture and Black Consciousness: Afro-American Folk Thought from Slavery to Freedom* (New York: Oxford University Press, 1977), p. 5.

12. This terminology comes from Sterling Stuckey, *Slave Culture Nationalist Theory and the Foundations of Black Americans.* (New York: Oxford University Press, 1987). The title of the introductory chapter in this very important book is "Slavery and the Circle of Culture." I believe that hermeneutics and culture are necessary correlates.

13. See Juan Luis Segundo, *Liberation of Theology,* trans. by John Drury, (Maryknoll, N. Y.: Orbis Books, 1976), p. 9. He says, "Firstly there is our way of experiencing reality which leads us to ideological suspicion. Secondly there is the application of our ideological suspicion to the whole ideological superstructure in general and to theology in particular. Thirdly there comes a new way of experiencing theological reality that leads us to exegetical suspicion, that is to the suspicion that the prevailing interpretation of the Bible has not taken important pieces of data into account. Fourthly we have our new hermeneutic, that is, our new way of interpreting the fountainhead of our faith (i.e., Scripture) with the new elements at our disposal" (p. 9).

14. See Justo L. and Catherine G. Gonzalez, *Liberation Preaching* (Nashville: Abingdon Press, 1980), p. 32.

15. Don Wardlaw, ed., *Preaching Biblically* (Philadelphia: Westminster Press, 1983), p. 16ff.

16. Ibid., p. 21.

17. Ibid., p. 21.

18. Cornel West, *Prophetic Fragments* (Grand Rapids: Eerdmans, 1988), p. 43.

19. E. Franklin Frazier in *The Negro Church in America* (New York: Schocken Books, 1964) is redundant in saying, "Through the medium of the negro preacher the stories in the Bible were dramatized for the negro and many characters and incidents were interpreted in terms of the negro experience" (p. 18). At another point, Frazier states, "Preaching meant dramatizing the stories of the Bible and the ways of God to man. These slave preachers were noted for the imagery of their sermons" (p. 24).

20. Ibid., p. 25.

21. James F. Hopewell, *Congregation: Stories and Structures* (Philadelphia: Fortress Press, 1987). Hopewell says, "The hermeneutical task is not merely the meaning of biblical revelation in ways meaningful to individuals. It is more basically the tuning of the complex discourse of the congregation so that the gospel sounds within the message of its many voices" (p. 11).

22. See, for example, Michael Gelvin: *A Commentary on Heidegger's Being and Time: A Section-by-Section Interpretation* (New York: Harper & Row, 1970), pp. 16ff.

23. John Macquarrie, *Martin Heidegger* (Richmond, Va.: John Knox Press, 1968).

24. Ibid., pp. 12 and 14.

25. Ibid., p. 62.

26. Stuckey, *Slave Culture*, p. 29.

27. Ibid., pp. 12, 19.

28. Ibid., pp. 94–95.

29. Macquarrie, *Heidegger,* p. 61.

30. William Barrett, *Irrational Man: A Study in Existential Philosophy* (New York: Doubleday/Anchor Books, 1958), p. 167.

31. Ibid., pp. 149–80.

32. Hans Gadamer, *Truth and Method* (New York: Seabury Press, 1975), p. 93.

33. Levine, *Black Culture and Black Consciousness*, p. 58.

34. Gadamer, *Truth and Method,* p. 100.

35. Ibid.

Chapter 4

1. Kenneth M. Jones, "The Black Male in Jeopardy: A Crisis Report on the Status of the Black American Male," *The Crisis Magazine* (March 1986), p. 18.

2. See William Ryan, *Blaming the Victim;* James Q. Wilson, *Varieties of Police Behavior: The Management of Law and Order in Eight Communities* (Cambridge: Harvard University Press, 1968); Nathan Glazer, *Affirmative Discrimination: Ethnic Inequality and Public Policy* (New York: Basic Books, 1975); and, Isabel V. Sawhill, "An Overview," and Daniel Patrick Moynihan, "Toward a Post-Industrial Social Policy," *The Public Interest,* no. 96 (Summer 1989), [Sawhill] pp. 3–15, [Moynihan] pp. 16–27.

3. See Reinhold Niebuhr, *The Nature and Destiny of Man: A Christian Interpretation,* vol. 1(New York: Charles Scribner's Sons, 1941).

4. See Jewelle Taylor Gibbs et al., eds., *Young, Black and Male in America* (Dover, Mass.: Auburn House, 1988).

5. John C. Gaston, "The Destruction of the Young Black Male: The Impact of Popular Culture and Organized Sports." *Journal of Black Studies,* vol. 16, no. 4 (June 1986), p. 371.

6. Ibid., p. 371.

7. Ray Marshall, Gibbs, ed., foreword to *Young, Black and Male in America,* p. xiv.

8. See Rodney Reed, "Education and Achievement of Young Black Males," in Gibbs, ed., *Young, Black Males in America.*

9. William Oliver, "Black Males and Social Problems: Prevention Through Afrocentric Socialization," *Journal of Black Studies,* vol. 20, no. 1 (September 1989), p. 21.

10. Ibid., p. 21–22.

11. See Molefi Kete Asante, *The Afrocentric Idea* (Philadelphia: Temple University Press, 1987), and J. Jahn, *Muntu: The New African Culture* (New York: Grove Press, 1961).

12. David J. Dent, "Readin', Writin', and Rage: How Schools Are Destroying Black Boys," *Essence* magazine, (November 1989), p. 54.

13. Ibid.

14. William Strickland, "The Future of Black Men," *Essence* magazine (November 1989), p. 51.

15. Ibid., p. 51.

16. Ruth Mitchell et al., "Tracking: Does It Derail Minorities?" *Virginia Journal of Education* (February 1990), p. 9.

17. See Reed, "Education and Achievement of Young Black Males," pp. 79–80.

18. See "Minority Achievement: Not Yet a Real Priority," *Virginia Journal of Education* (February 1990), p. 21.

19. Michelle Collison, "More Young Black Men Choosing Not to Go to College" *The Chronicle of Higher Education*, vol. XXXIV, no. 15 (December 9, 1987), p. A1.

20. Ibid., p. A27.

21. Friere, *Pedagogy of the Oppressed* (New York: Seabury Press, 1972), p. 39.

22. Collison, "More Young Black Men Choosing Not to Go to College," A1, A17.

23. Richard Dembo, "Delinquency among Black Male Youth," in Gibbs, ed., *Young, Black and Male in America*, p. 132.

24. Ibid., p. 138.

25. See Dembo, "Delinquency among Black Male Youth," in Gibbs, ed., *Young, Black and Male in America* and Robert J. Sampson, "Urban Black Violence: The Effect of Male Joblessness and Family Disruption," *American Journal of Sociology*, vol. 93, no. 3 (September 1987), pp. 348–82.

26. See Thomas A. Parham and Roderick J. McDavis, "Black Men, an Endangered Species: Who's Really Pulling the Trigger?" *The Journal of Counseling and Development*, vol. 66 (September 1987), p. 24.

27. Ibid., p. 25.

28. See "Why Black Men Have the Highest Cancer Rate," *Ebony* (March 1983), pp. 69, 72.

29. Ibid., p. 69.

30. See Sar Levitan and Isaac Shapiro, *Working, but Poor* (Baltimore: Johns Hopkins University Press), 1987.

31. Ernest Spaight and Harold E. Dixon, "Black Youth Unemployment," *The Journal of Black Studies*, vol. 16, no. 4 (June 1986), p. 386.

Chapter 5

1. See Ezra P. Gould, *The Gospel According to St. Mark*. The International Critical Commentary (New York: Charles Scribners' Sons, 1986), p. 90

Annotated Bibliography

Baldwin, Lewis V. *There Is a Balm in Gilead*. Minneapolis: Fortress Press, 1991. A book on the life of Dr. Martin Luther King Jr. and his influence on the liberation struggle of black people. While it does not directly deal with preaching, King was first and foremost a preacher who understood the transformative nature of the gospel.

Boff, Leonardo, and Clodovis Boff. *Introducing Liberation Theology*. Maryknoll, N.Y.: Orbis Books, 1987. An introduction to the concept of liberation theology. It gives a nontechnical and objective account of this theological practice.

Brueggemann, Walter. *Finally Comes the Poet*. Minneapolis: Fortress Press, 1989. Addresses the crisis of interpretation, which has either dismissed or controlled the text, that the preacher faces in our culture.

Buttrick, David G. *Preaching Jesus Christ*. Philadelphia: Fortress Press, 1988. Focuses on the life, message, death, and resurrection of Christ, as well as the problems of preaching Christology to our present society.

Claypool, John R. *The Preaching Event*. San Francisco: Harper & Row, 1990. Deals with "confessional preaching" and how the preacher's story can get in the way of the Great Story and deflect attention to the wrong place.

Cone, James H. *For My People*. Maryknoll, N. Y.: Orbis Books, 1984. Addresses the full range of factors in North American religion that make for the traditional black church/white church dichotomy.

Craddock, Fred B. *Overhearing the Gospel*. Nashville: Abingdon Press, 1986. Examines the problem of effectively preaching the word of God to persons who have "heard it all before." It addresses the causes, prevention, and cure, and exposes common illusions and attitudes that block effective communication of the gospel.

Craddock, Fred B. *Preaching*. Nashville: Abingdon Press, 1985. Answers the fundamental question, How does one prepare and deliver a sermon? It provides an intelligible guide to sermon preparation and additionally allows for concentrated study of any particular dimension of the process.

Davis, Gerald L. *I Got the Word in Me and I Can Sing It, You Know.*

Philadelphia: University of Pennsylvania Press, 1987. Deals with the description, definition, and analysis of the oral formulas and structural units in the performed sermon.

Fant, Clyde E. *Bonhoeffer: Wordly Preaching.* Nashville: Thomas Nelson, 1975. A classic in the study of homiletics.

Felder, Cain H. *Troubling Biblical Waters.* Maryknoll, N.Y.: Orbis Books, 1989. This landmark study presents a new hermeneutical approach to biblical study and understanding. Felder suggests that the traditional Eurocentric view of the Bible fails to adequately address the liberation motif that is necessary to fully understanding the Bible.

Forbes, James. *The Holy Spirit and Preaching.* Nashville: Abingdon Press, 1989. Forbes focuses on the Holy Spirit as it relates to preaching. He demonstrates how the Holy Spirit works with the pastor in the preparation and delivery of a sermon and concludes by focusing on the need for anointed preaching and the way anointed preaching happens today.

Gonzalez, Justo L., and Catherine G. Gonzalez. *Liberation Preaching.* Nashville: Abingdon Press, 1984. Provides an effective introduction to liberation theology from the preaching perspective. It is a landmark publication—essentially the first of its kind.

Harris, James H. *Pastoral Theology.* Minneapolis: Fortress Press, 1991. Deals with a practical aspect of church life. Harris's chapter on preaching and worship gives a brief outline of liberation themes.

Keck, Leander E. *The Bible in the Pulpit.* Nashville: Abingdon Press, 1986. Keck examines the whys and wherefores of biblical preaching and its inseparable connections with the pulpit.

Lischer, Richard. *Theories of Preaching: Selected Readings in the Homiletical Tradition.* Durham: Labyrinth Press, 1987. This book is a composite of the thought of several outstanding preachers and theologians. It is composed of selected readings from the homiletics tradition going back to Phillips Brooks and ending with contemporaries such as Geoffrey Wainwright and Fred Craddock. It includes selections from Henry Mitchell and W.E.B. Du Bois.

Long, Thomas G. *Preaching and the Literary Forms of the Bible.* Philadelphia: Fortress Press, 1989. Long argues that the literary form and dynamics of biblical texts can and should make a difference in the kinds of sermons created from those texts.

Long, Thomas G., and Neely McCarter, editors. *Preaching In and*

Out of Season. Louisville: Westminster/John Knox Press, 1990. A collection of essays on preaching as it relates to racial relations, family, church, stewardship, evangelism. An excellent resource for preaching and worship.

MacLeod, Donald. *The Problem of Preaching.* Philadelphia: Fortress Press, 1987. Addresses the contemporary preacher's recurring problem: Who and what am I?

Mitchell, Henry H. *Celebration and Experience in Preaching.* Nashville: Abingdon Press, 1990. In this book, Mitchell shows how to use imagination, emotive expressions, and the sermon celebrations to meet the emotional and rational needs of people in the congregation.

————. *The Recovery of Preaching.* San Francisco: Harper & Row, 1977. Meets the need to join the preacher with the people in the pews by preaching for a single tradition and applying its insights to the preaching situation in general.

Proctor, Samuel D. *Preaching about Crisis in the Community.* Philadelphia: Westminster Press, 1988. Focuses on the essential link between the gospel message and the problems of society. Proctor illustrates how this kind of preaching involves making a serious response to problems such as drug abuse, homelessness, and so on. Proctor describes and demonstrates the dialectical method, drawing upon the basic ideas and philosophical constructs of G. W. F. Hegel.

Raboteau, Albert J. *Slave Religion.* New York: Oxford University Press, 1978. This book is a documented history explaining in detail the religious life of the slaves. Raboteau seeks to answer questions such as, What were the origins of Black religion in America? What aspects of African religion were retained by the slaves? What was the nature of the religion to which the slave was converted? An excellent historical source.

Red, David H. C. *Preaching about the Needs of Real People.* Philadelphia: Westminster Press, 1988. Discusses contemporary biblical preaching and its potential for reaching people at the point of their real needs, whether those needs concern loneliness, marital problems, or global crisis.

Stapleton, John M. Preaching in *Demonstration of Spirit and Power.* Philadelphia: Fortress Press, 1988. This book expresses the author's interest in ascertaining how we may preach "in demonstration of the Spirit and of Power." His section on Christology is most illuminating.

Stuckey, Sterling. *Slave Culture.* New York: Oxford Press, 1987. This book deals with how the problem of cultural self-definition must be resolved among African Americans, especially in regard to their Africanness, if black liberation is to be achieved. Stuckey's book is a masterpiece, and essential reading for understanding slavery and the slave preacher.

Thulin, Richard L. *The "I" of the Sermon.* Minneapolis: Fortress Press, 1989. Thulin focuses on four types of personal stories: illustration, reminiscence, confession, and self-portrayal. He describes the essential components of each type and demonstrates how each can "proclaim Christ" and accurately express the biblical text. He suggests ways that the tellers of personal stories can avoid narcissism, primatism, and the isolated tale.

Thurman, Howard. *Jesus and the Disinherited.* Richmond, Ind.: Friends United Press, 1976. Thurman interprets Jesus' message for the oppressed of today and exposes the isolation and destructive forces of fear, deception, and hatred, and suggests the love ethic of Jesus as a difficult but essential way to overcome the destructive nature of oppression.

Van Seters, Arthur, ed. *Preaching as a Social Act.* Nashville: Abingdon Press, 1988. A comprehensive examination of the way in which society influences preaching and the way that preaching can influence society.

Wardlaw, Don M. *Preaching Biblically.* Philadelphia: Westminster Press, 1983. This book defends the thesis that the sermon's form should duplicate the forms of the text. An excellent resource on biblical hermeneutics.

White, Richard C. *Biblical Preaching.* St. Louis: LBP Press, 1988. This book deals with interpreting the text for our current conditions by listening to the divine voice of God.

Williamson, William H. *Preaching about Conflict in the Local Church.* Philadelphia: Westminster Press, 1987. This book discusses how to prepare sermons on controversial subjects, suggesting ways to use the biblical text to examine divisive issues. Williamson's comments on the importance of style and delivery when dealing with difficult topics are very illuminating.

Wilson, Paul S. *Imagination of the Heart.* Nashville: Abingdon Press, 1988. Focuses on the development of a method for biblical preaching that incorporates the use of imagination, how Scripture and personal experiences can be used to train the imagination, and how this can both strengthen and enliven the task of preaching.

Index

Scripture Index